£.4.25

£ 2.85

# JOSEPH HAYDN

His Life in Contemporary Pictures

# JOSEPH HAYDN

## His Life in Contemporary Pictures

COLLECTED AND SUPPLIED
WITH A COMMENTARY AND AN
ICONOGRAPHY OF AUTHENTIC HAYDN PICTURES
BY
LÁSZLÓ SOMFAI

FABER AND FABER
24 RUSSELL SQUARE
LONDON

First published in England in 1969
by Faber and Faber Limited
24 Russell Square, London W C 1
© Faber and Faber Ltd., London and
Corvina Press, Budapest
Cover: Joseph Haydn, portrait by Ludwig Seehas, 1785
(State Museum, Schwerin)

Translated by Mari Kuttna and Károly Ravasz
Binding and cover design by Klára Pap
Printed in Hungary 1969
Kossuth Printing House, Budapest

TO THE MEMORY OF OTTO ERICH DEUTSCH

# FOREWORD

Of the three great Viennese classics, Haydn was the last to have his life and works thoroughly examined and edited. Even today there is no complete list of his compositions and the complete critical edition is still in preparation. A scholarly edition of his collected letters and notes was only recently published in the original language (Budapest/Kassel etc. 1965, Bärenreiter—Corvina). But many years may yet elapse before a comprehensive and fundamental modern Haydn monograph appears.

Nor has the pictorial documentation been systematically and completely collected yet, which is the more regrettable since the losses which have occurred, mainly in the devastation of the Second World War, can no longer be made good. Even if its size does make this book appear not unimportant, it is still, when measured against the seventy-seven years of Haydn's life, a rather modest volume and not a finite collection of pictures of all the events of his life. A scholarly summary similar to the exemplary Mozart picture volume, published in 1961,* can only be created on the basis of international co-operation taking perhaps several decades.

The idea of this book originated during the Haydn memorial year of 1959. The international meeting on musicology in Budapest, along with several publications, directed attention to the Haydn documents in Hungary. The pictorial and documentary material available here would fill a comprehensive, independent volume on *Haydn in Hungary*, since the master spent almost three decades of his life on Hungarian soil in the service of the Hungarian Prince Esterházy. The Esterházy Archives, which have been housed since 1948 in public collections in Budapest, provide further rich source material. Yet, for two reasons, this book attempts to go beyond these limits. First, any restrictive selection of the material would destroy the continuity of time and space, and would present a distorted picture of Haydn's life and work. Secondly, the impression could be created that today's Hungarian musicologists were presenting some special claim on Haydn, or wished to over-emphasize his connections with Hungary.

The richest Haydn picture album to date** also indicates that the contemporary documents about Haydn's life are not very abundant. There are some missing links that can no longer be forged. In particular, few Haydn portraits have survived. Except for one picture of the thirty-five-year-old Haydn, of little artistic value and questionable authenticity, all the extant portraits show Haydn after his fiftieth year. Pictures of Haydn's parents are missing, probably because cartwright Haydn and his wife were simple, quiet people. Unfortunately, there are no authentic portraits either of Haydn's wife or of the several women who were close to him, such as Luigia Polzelli, Frau von Genzinger and Mrs. Schroeter. Pictures of his contemporaries, of the lovers and promoters of his music, are also missing. Haydn had not seen much of the world, he knew little of Europe, and, apart from Austria and Hungary, lived only in England for a longer period. It was quite different with Wolfgang Amadeus Mozart: either his father or his mother accompanied him on his numerous journeys, and in letters home they wrote about his various experiences. Haydn has left only incomplete notes about his relatively short journeys to London. And since we do not wish to make assumptions or repeat legends, we have to be satisfied with the fact that no search, however long, will lead us to documents as full and comprehensive as are available about Mozart's life and works, the collection of which began much earlier and in much more favourable circumstances.

The uneven number of pictures available of contemporaries close to Haydn determines the modest size of this book. In order to keep to the chronological presentation of the

*Mozart and His World in Contemporary Pictures.* Initiated by Maximilian Zenger. Presented by Otto Erich Deutsch, Bärenreiter, 1961.
**Richard Petzoldt—Edouard Crass: *Joseph Haydn. Sein Leben in Bildern.* Leipzig, 1959, with 111 pictures.

most important events, we forego the presentation of facts of minor importance, even if more illustrations of these could be shown. To preserve the sense of proportion of the biography, we have not presented his journey to Britain in greater detail, although here his notebooks would have offered opportunities to select more illustrations of people, towns and buildings known to Haydn. Our book ends with Haydn's death. A report of his funeral, of his skull, which was lost and recovered a long time later, and the assembling of his mortal remains, would be an impious offence against the respect and esteem which posterity owes to this great musician. Neither do we show pictures of towns from which Haydn received letters. We show only what Haydn himself had seen. The 'white spots' in the biography are best filled by facsimiles of his manuscripts, which show the development of Haydn's musical style.

An iconography based on authentic pictures of Haydn which have been assembled chronologically in the book, seemed essential. It is this side of his work, which continues the earlier experiments of Vogel, Marcel, Schnerich, Botstieber, Muller, et alii, that the author feels to be of special value. The restriction to 'contemporary' pictorial material presented special problems. Whenever a picture of Haydn's time could not be found or was not accessible, the pictures of Haydn's contemporaries, the views of towns and buildings, sometimes originate from earlier or later years. Photographs have been used only of objects such as statues, reliefs, musical instruments and memorials. Photographs of buildings were eschewed, even where no contemporary pictures existed. This reduces the number of pictures, but a photographic reproduction would have an aesthetically disturbing effect in this framework.

For the sake of authenticity, the text which links the pictorial documents and the biographical data is taken, wherever possible, from Haydn's correspondence and from his Notebooks, as well as from his first biographies by Griesinger and Dies. The English translation of the former is by H. C. Robbins Landon* and of the latter by Vernon Gotwals.**

It is a pleasant duty to express my sincere thanks to those who helped me with this work, both individuals and institutions. In addition to the libraries, museums, collections and colleagues and friends individually listed in my sources, the following few at least must be mentioned: In the Haydn-city of Vienna, the late Professor Otto Erich Deutsch, whom I was able to consult repeatedly about the Haydn iconography; Mrs. Christa Landon, who gave her invaluable support in collecting the material and in revising the second edition of the book; Dr. Franz Glück, Director of the Historisches Museum der Stadt Wien; Dr. Hedwig Mitringer, Archivist of the Gesellschaft der Musikfreunde; —in England, Mrs. Eva Alberman, London; Mr. Oliver Davies, Royal College of Music, London; Dr. Richard Friedenthal, London; Mr. O. W. Neighbour, of the Music Room of the British Museum; Mr. Donald Mitchell and Mr. John M. Thomson, of the Music Department, Faber and Faber Ltd., London;—further, Professor Dénes Bartha, Budapest; Dr. Johann Harich, formerly curator of the Esterházy Archives, Vienna; Dr. H. C. Anthony van Hoboken, Ascona; Mr. H. C. Robbins Landon, Buggiano—Vienna; Professor Jens Peter Larsen, Copenhagen; Dr. Wolfgang Rehm, Kassel; Mr. László Sarlós, Budapest; Dr. C. G. Stellan-Mörner, Stockholm; Dr. Volker von Volckamer, Harburg Castle;—the Corvina Publishing House, Budapest and Faber and Faber Ltd., London;—and finally quite special thanks to Mrs. Dorrit Révész-Somfai, without whose help and encouragement this book could never have been completed.

Budapest, summer 1968

*László Somfai*

*The Collected Correspondence and London Notebooks of Joseph Haydn*, Barrie and Rockliff, London, 1959.
**Joseph Haydn, Eighteenth-Century Gentleman and Genius*. A translation with introduction and notes by Vernon Gotwals of the *Biographische Notizen über Joseph Haydn* by G. A. Griesinger and the *Biographische Nachrichten von Joseph Haydn* by A. C. Dies, University of Wisconsin Press, Madison, 1963.

# CONTENTS

# JOSEPH HAYDN
## HIS APPEARANCE, CHARACTER
## AND MUSICAL CAREER

'Haydn was small in stature, but sturdy and strongly built. His forehead was broad and well modelled, his skin brown, his eyes bright and fiery, his other features full and strongly marked, and his whole physiognomy and bearing bespoke prudence and a quiet gravity'—wrote Georg August Griesinger in his description. Albert Christoph Dies added: 'The lower half of his body was too short for the upper, something commonly to be seen in small persons of either sex, but very noticeable in Haydn because he kept to the old fashion of having his trousers reach only to the hips and not above the waist. His features were fairly regular; his look was eloquent, fiery, but still moderate, kind, attractive... His hawk's nose (he suffered much from a nasal polyp, which had doubtless enlarged this part) and other features as well were heavily pock-marked, the nose even seemed so that the nostrils each had a different shape.'

All this explains why Haydn himself never commissioned a portrait, and why most artists who painted him even falsified his traits, though perhaps unintentionally, in their idealisation of him. Unfortunately, these artists included only one of note: John Hoppner. Nevertheless, the death mask and the agreement of certain characteristic features in the portraits make it possible to reconstruct Haydn's features in an authentic way, at least in the most important traits. The heads of those portraits which seem to be most trustworthy have been compared for such an experiment (see pages XIV—XV). This not over-attractive face was hardly likely to impress Haydn's contemporaries, or to make them suspect that they were facing a man of outstanding genius.

Haydn's spiritual attitude and his character had no obscure or puzzling elements. He was simple, unconstrained and natural, and he was far more so than any other important personality in the history of music. His origins no doubt played a decisive part in this. As the offspring of peasants and craftsmen, he was the first to span by his own exertions the gap which is usually only filled by several generations: from the slumbering consciousness of simple people living by the work of their own hands, through the transitional stage of passive education to the educated, self-conscious, creative artist. This quick rise took place without any psychological or social conflicts. Through all the periods of his life, it could not even have occurred to Haydn, who had risen from the lowest station to social heights, to break the feudal fetters of his position. Even after the already loosened bonds of his dependence had been completely dissolved, he felt himself constrained by custom and descent and burdened by memories, and did not consider himself to belong to the bourgeoisie. Free from bonds of status, he was able to spend his old age in an unrestricted independence of mind and spirit. His childlessness probably further strengthened his sense of independence.

His mental attitudes and his character were decisively determined by his peasant simplicity and unconstrained piety. 'Haydn was very religiously inclined and was loyally devoted to the faith in which he was raised... All his larger scores begin with the words: *In nomine Domini* and end with *Laus Deo* or *Soli Deo gloria* [In the name of the Lord, Praise to God, To God alone the glory]... This instance, however, does not indicate intolerant feelings. Haydn left every man to his own conviction and recognized all as brothers. In general, his devotion was not of the gloomy, always suffering sort, but rather cheerful and reconciled, and in this character, moreover, he wrote all his church music... A natural consequence of Haydn's religiosity was his modesty, for his talent was not of his own doing, rather a gracious gift from Heaven, to whom he believed he must show himself thankful. Once the clavier-player ... from P. visited him. "You are Haydn, the great Haydn," he began with theatrical bearing. "One should fall on his knees before you! One should approach you only as a being of the highest sort!"—"Oh my dear sir," countered Haydn. "don't talk to me like that. Consider me a man whom God has granted talent and a good heart. I push my claims no further."—"Do you know what bothers me?"—the visitor went on, when he had looked around the room. "You should live in the most splendid palace, your garden should be ten times larger, you should drive with six horses, live in the circles of the great."—"All that," countered Haydn, "is not in keeping with my wishes; I had a hard time in my youth, and I strove even then to earn enough to be free of care in my old days. In this I succeeded, thank God. I have my own comfortable house, three or four courses at dinner, a good glass of wine, I can dress well, and when I want to drive out, a hired coach is good enough for me. I have associated with emperors, kings and many great gentlemen, and have heard many flattering things from them; but I do not wish to live on intimate footing with such persons, and I prefer people of my own status." ' (Griesinger)

'A harmless roguery, or what the British call *humour*, was one of Haydn's outstanding characteristics. He easily and by preference discovered the comic side of anything, and anyone who had spent even an hour with him must have noticed that the very spirit of Austrian cheerfulness breathed in him.' (Griesinger) This trait of his character is just as well known as his passion for order, which was remarkable throughout his life. Friends who visited him in his old age praised the tidiness of his house and of his personal possessions. Even when he had become very frail, he was always well dressed to receive his visitors. He was a careful observer who remarked on everything that happened around him with an almost fussy exactitude. The most diverse notes are to be found in his London Notebooks: on horseraces, towns and buildings, then a recipe for a punch, statistical data and a conservation procedure for milk; then he writes about battleships in Portsmouth, reports on the social standing and financial situation of his patrons, the scandalous private lives of artists, describes the characteristic British type, tells stories that are going around; and all this with biting irony and very much to the point. He certainly observed the peculiarities of the world which was new and unknown to him with special attention, because in his earlier years he seldom found time and opportunities for such free and easy pleasures. 'Hunting and fishing were Haydn's favourite pastimes during his stay in Hungary, and he never forgot that he once brought down with one shot three hazel-hens, which appeared on the table of the Empress Maria Theresa... In riding Haydn developed no skill, because after he had fallen from a horse on the Morzin estates, he never again trusted himself to mount.' (Griesinger)

Three less important characteristics which make him appear perhaps in a less attractive light can also be traced to his healthy peasant mentality. His extra-marital relations could be understood by anyone who knew his unbearable wife. But the sentence by which Haydn acquitted himself stated that: '...my wife was unable to bear children, and I was therefore less indifferent to the charms of other ladies.' (Griesinger) His other very human weakness, richly documented in his letters, was the crafty haggling with his publishers: this was even more excusable and justifiable, since in those days when there were as yet no copyright laws, he could make money from only a fraction of his gigantic output. His alleged avarice is mentioned as the third weakness in his character. This rumour originates from visitors to Haydn in his old age, who were expecting to meet a romantic artist and hero. Of course, they were bound to be disappointed. Albert Christoph Dies writes of this: 'I had occasion enough to investigate this accusation and found it false. Avarice has no feeling for the need of others, and does not even support its closest kin... If Haydn had need of money, he was very industrious in earning it, but once it was earned and in his hands, he felt the inclination to share it.' He was not avaricious, only economical, as were his peasant ancestors, who also gave thought to the morrow. This too explains the childish joy he often displayed on receiving the precious souvenirs he was given by his princely patrons. In spite of his austerity, he was always ready to assist relatives and friends in want with gifts of money. That he was proud of his charity and expected to be thanked for it cannot be held against a man who felt flattered at having got so far by his own work that he was able to be generous.'

If we try to get acquainted with Haydn's character from his statements and notes, we must remember that beyond the narrow confines of music he was not really an educated man. This was a result of his circumstances. He did not even speak his German mother tongue in its standard form. 'Haydn spoke in broad Austrian dialect, and his conversation was richly endowed with that comic and naive manner of speaking peculiar to the Austrians. He had little facility in the French language, but he spoke Italian readily and fluently. In English he had learned during his two journeys to express himself at a pinch, and in Latin he understood everything in that tongue in the Catholic ritual.' (Griesinger)

He also lacked the time and the opportunities to give himself a literary education, or to study the fine arts. In this he resembled most important musicians of his time. Likewise, works of literature were not to be found in his library; instead, there were books waiting to be set to music. Most surprisingly, the performance of a Shakespeare tragedy which he once attended in England did not rate a mention in his notes, whereas he transcribed many valueless poems and rhymes. Haydn was naively helpless in the selection of the poets for his choral and vocal works. In Haydn's letters and memoirs, there is no mention of the Goethe, Lessing and Shakespeare plays performed yearly in the Esterházy theatre. What impressed him in England about buildings, memorials or paintings was not their artistic value, but their unusual size or tremendous production costs. Science and philosophy were to him a closed book. After a visit to the well-known English astronomer, Herschel, in Slough, he wrote in his diary with childish amazement of the tools and instruments previously unknown to him, their price and the adventurous life of their creator. The outstanding achievements in philosophy in his lifetime, the thoughts of Kant and Rousseau, remained unknown to him.

At a time when Europe was in ferment and the existing social order was beginning to totter, in the years of upheaval that led to the French Revolution, he went on living quietly, taking sides with no political party whatever. No action or statement of his is recorded that shows political relevance or even awareness. Although he read the newspapers regularly in his old age, there is nothing to show that he understood the importance of the Paris Revolution of 1789, or its political and social effects. On his two visits to England, on the journeys out and back, he avoided the increasingly restless city of Paris, although an enthusiastic public would have celebrated him there. But the Austrian rebellion of 1796, which arose from the fear of Napoleon's advance, moved him to offer his compositions freely for welfare concerts. He created his 'Gott erhalte', the song that became a national anthem: in his old age he played it daily to himself on the piano with deep feeling. He accepted the recognition of kings with great satisfaction, without ever becoming subservient. He never adopted revolutionary attitudes, although in his London diaries he noted with acute perception many of the shortcomings of bourgeois society: abuses in the administration of justice, the exploitation of apprentices, the ridiculous dogmatism of the high clergy of the Anglican Church and of the Quakers, the immorality of society, the misery of minor musicians, and many other things.

But how could he have acquired an insight into the world of the arts, the sciences, the newest political endeavours? The knowledge gained from his schooling in Hainburg and Vienna was limited almost exclusively to the Catechism and to Latin grammar. Nobody taught him to understand or to appreciate literature and the fine arts. The much-travelled and knowledgeable foreigners who visited Eszterháza saw in Haydn only a court employee who had to look after their musical entertainment, and who neither dared nor tried to approach gentlemen of high standing. The attention of well-known Viennese patrons of the arts such as Kees, Durazzo, van Swieten and others was probably directed only to his music. The few Viennese families who already in 1780 considered it an honour to entertain Haydn as a guest, had only one topic in common with him: music. His cordial relationship with the music-loving family of the physician Genzinger did not contribute to the extension of Haydn's education, though it presented him with the warmth of a home, tender love and care. In London, and in the last years of his life he met with unprecedented esteem, but his visitors did not look to him as a conversationalist, rather as an object for their admiration. 'When Lord Nelson travelled through Vienna, he asked for a worn-out pen that Haydn had used in his composing, and made him a present of his watch in return. Haydn had Maret, Soult and several eminent French officers who were in Vienna at the end of the year 1805, and visited him, inscribe their names in a book; and on days when he felt well, he generally welcomed visits from strangers travelling by.' (Griesinger)

See Iconography
of Authentic Haydn
Pictures
Nos. 3, 8B
Nos. 9, 12
Nos. 10A, 11A

See Iconography
of Authentic Haydn
Pictures
Nos. 15A, 18
Nos. 16, 17B
Nos. 19, 23

From quite early on, the world saw him exclusively as the great musician. This limited his friends and acquaintances to a narrow circle. Most of the musicians who were on close terms with him for many years—Dittersdorf, Albrechtsberger, Salomon, Tomasini and Hummel—were likewise mostly one-sided in their education. This also applied to his favourite pupils, Pleyel, Neukomm and others. Haydn lived long enough to see Count von Harrach, in whose house his mother had served as a maid, erect a memorial in his honour in the village of his birth. Poets praised him in their poems, and the compositions dedicated to him are innumerable. But he had never found a friend and equal who could have drawn his attention, in a friendly way, to the shortcomings in his education and given him a helping hand.

Haydn's attitudes were always unequivocal; his views on contemporaries, on musicians, on all the events of his age were always clear, without ambivalence and without contradiction. Yet there were two aspects of Haydn's life that seem less simple: the change in his personality from the submissive letters to the Prince in the sixties, to the rebellious ones prior to his journey to England—although Haydn returned to the service of Prince Esterházy after tasting the life of a free musician—and the question of the extent to which Haydn's friendship for Mozart was sincere. Both these questions deserve closer examination.

When, at the age of seventeen, he was obliged to support himself by means of his knowledge of music, he sought and found support and work from noble patrons, and later, employment, which enabled him to fill in the gaps in his musical education through practical work, and to mature into an artist. In some ways he was rather cunning and guileful; he worked very hard so that his master, the Prince, would forgive his small 'breaches of contract'—the increasing number of works he composed and had published as outside commissions. One should disregard the obligatory courtesies in his letters and requests. Besides his humble expressions of thanks, his requests, diplomatically-worded demands and assertions of self-confidence soon became more frequent. During the years 1770–1790 the relationship of master to servant between the Prince and his conductor acquired a new note: the person of Prince Nikolaus, the Magnificent, became an increasingly stronger link in the chain that bound Haydn to the residence than the original severe contract. One could almost call their relationship a friendship. In many respects Haydn owed the Prince a personal debt of gratitude until the death of the latter relieved him of this moral obligation. He was granted a chance to experience the free life of an artist. Prince Nikolaus's less highly esteemed successor continued to accord Haydn his conductor's salary. Haydn acknowledged this splendid gesture with letters that were blunt, laconic, barely polite: yet he returned to the princely family after his second journey to England. There is one opinion frequently quoted about his return which needs correcting. As mentioned above, relations with the Esterházys had not been severed completely even during the years 1781—1795. However, when Haydn returned to Vienna, he did not assume precisely those obligations which he had renounced in 1790. His employment became, in a sense, 'formal'. From then on he was spared humiliations over money, while he received a salary to assure his carefree old age. It was a kind of pension for his services over thirty years. He probably did not consider his title of 'Conductor to Prince Esterházy' belittling, as the musical life of the Esterházy residence had, under his leadership, become famous throughout Europe. It is likely that he felt it an honour to hold the title which he bore to the end of his life. Posterity may draw its conclusions about Haydn's relationship with Mozart from a few laconic statements. Above all, a letter from Leopold Mozart and the measured but enthusiastic words of esteem in a letter from Haydn to Prague, which are known from a published copy, justify the assumption that Haydn honestly considered that this friendship did him honour. Similarly, the words with which Mozart dedicated his six quartets (K. 387, 421, 428, 458, 464, 465) to Haydn are proof of this friendship. Yet a few acrimonious and ironic remarks uttered by Mozart from time to time, which probably grieved Haydn, then in London, make one wonder. Besides, Haydn once (in 1789) simply deleted an aria that Mozart had composed for an Anfossi opera. It is surprising, moreover, that Haydn did not allow a single one of Mozart's highly praised operas to be performed at Eszterháza; but this may be explained by the small operatic ensemble there. Some jealousy may have been lurking behind their friendship and mutual esteem. This may also be explained by the considerable difference in their ages and the unequal pace of their musical development, as well as by the fundamental dissimilarity of their natures. Haydn was incomparably simpler, kinder and less perplexing: he was more reticent in speaking and writing, more prudish in his humour and in his attitude to life, but then his education had been entirely different from Mozart's.

It can be seen that Haydn's life, as disclosed by biographical data, documents and pictures, moved in narrow confines. To what extent was Haydn swept along in the stream of historical and social events? To what extent was his personality formed by his age, how much did he contribute to the cultural developments of his period? In considering only his private life, only actions that are susceptible to analysis, we obtain little by way of answer to these questions. Haydn's epoch-making genius manifested itself exclusively in his music. It is in his art therefore that we must seek the key to his innermost self. His greatest joy was to make people happy through his music. 'Often, when struggling against the obstacles of every sort which oppose my labours; often, when the powers of mind and body weakened and it was difficult for me to continue in the course I had entered on; a secret voice whispered to me: "There are so few happy and contented peoples here below; grief and sorrow are always their lot; perhaps your labours will once be a source from which the care-worn, or the man burdened with affairs, can derive a few moments' rest and refreshment." This was indeed a powerful motive to press onwards, and this is why I now look back with cheerful satisfaction on the labours expended on this art, to which I have devoted so many long years of uninterrupted effort and exertion.' (From Haydn's letter to his admirers on the Island of Rügen, 22 September, 1802.)

The fifty years of musical development of which Haydn was creatively and decisively the leader were one of the most important turning-points in the history of music. He contributed to the overwhelming change in the language of music and in the forms of instrumental music. Haydn's first considerable composition that survived, the *Missa Brevis*, in F major, was probably written in 1750, the same year in which J. S. Bach wrote *The Art of Fugue* and in which he died. Haydn's last, uncompleted composition, two movements of the string quartet opus 103 (Hoboken III: 83) was written in 1803, the year in which Beethoven worked on his *Eroica*. These two compositions, *The Art of Fugue* and the *Eroica*, are landmarks in the decisive change in music that occurred in the half century from Bach to Beethoven. The period brought a conscious rejection of the polyphony which had been the rule; the great common themes and experiences (such as the protestant chorale, the Passion, the Biblical oratorio, the anthem in celebration of victory) were relegated to the background. The subjective composition of lively and sophisticated melodies began—a development which was to end in the dissolution of the classical order which had arisen in the meantime, and of the romantic re-appraisal which had been driven to its extreme in an experiment to represent collective movements and revolutions musically (examples of the latter are the song of the French Revolution and the 'liberation opera'; Beethoven's *Eroica* also belongs to these in essence), or by the interpretation of lyricism, the microcosm of subjective sentiments (songs, character pieces for solo instruments, etc.). During these fifty years, the number of people who wanted to listen to music, or wanted to play it, multiplied greatly. In all the larger cities of Europe public concerts began to be arranged, at which a new audience began to appear: the townsman who also wanted to listen to or practise music in his own home. As the function of music was extended, its importance increased. Musical works frequently acquired an intellectual or political influence, even inspiring political action, so perhaps for the first time in Europe, music became the leading art form. The most important, and, from the point of view of cultural history, most characteristic masterpieces of the period were musical works.
Opinions may differ on whether the turning-point in the history of music should be set at 1750, the year J. S. Bach died. One should not forget that in Italy as early as

HAYDN'S SIGNATURES
FROM HIS MUSICAL
MANUSCRIPTS
ORIGINAL SIZE
LEFT: FROM THE YEARS
1760, 1766, 1790
RIGHT: DEC. 1. 1767,
1796, 1802

1733, a year after Haydn was born, *La Serva padrona* by Pergolesi had been performed, and soon the orchestral music of Sammartini's generation succeeded the marvellous creations of baroque music. A new style began to prevail, which—although plain and artless at first—had more meaning for contemporaries than the old masterpieces of baroque art. In 1740 revolutionary attempts were still made in Mannheim to find a more popular, simpler, and yet more sentimental and dynamic musical language.

But Haydn's musical career began around 1750, in the environment of the then still provincial Viennese musical life. It seems fairly certain that, at the time of his studies and of his first musical experiments, he knew nothing of either the Italian or the Mannheim radical trends. The church music of Fux, Caldara, Bonno and the younger Reutter brought the baroque style close to Haydn, even if not on the highest level. Developing from the Austrian 'pre-classical' instrumental music of Wagenseil, Monn and others, Haydn learnt little about these new Mannheim experiments. The Haydn compositions that have survived from the 1750s were the first attempts of a gifted young man who nevertheless spoke in a provincial idiom. But these first attempts earned him the favour of the Viennese public, the same which had esteemed the generation of Reutter and Wagenseil. This public was not homogeneous by any means; but then, neither was the musical style and social attitude of the young Haydn entirely consistent. Although the aristocracy were still to be considered the most important patrons of music, bourgeois music-lovers were beginning to be significant as an audience. In Haydn's style, together with the 'educated' baroque music, there were sounds of Viennese divertimentos and also of the 'Gassenhauers' [street-songs].

How did Haydn develop from the vacillating uncertainty of his early musical career into the most deliberate composer of his time, one who made the most decisive contribution to the creation of classical Viennese music? If we search for the driving forces of Haydn's career, appearing, as it does, to contradict the universal laws of progress, it becomes obvious that it was precisely Haydn's restricted life which influenced the development of his style so favourably, and through him influenced Viennese classical music.

HAYDN'S SIGNATURES
TAKEN FROM RECEIPTS,
DOCUMENTS, LETTERS
ORIGINAL SIZE
LEFT: FROM THE YEARS
1762, 1771, 1806
RIGHT: 1766, 1805, 1808

What could a very talented musician achieve in the middle of the eighteenth century, who did not have the opportunity to undertake concert tours abroad? Concert tours in those days were also a means to studying abroad. ('I was a wizard on no instrument, but I knew the strength and the working of all; I was not a bad clavier-player or singer, and could also play a concerto on the violin,' quotes Griesinger.) It was Haydn's good fortune that even at an early age he could make his living as a conductor in a prince's establishment; that an orchestra consisting of good musicians was at his disposal. Thus he was not only able to experiment freely in composing all kinds of secular and ecclesiastical instrumental and vocal music but had to prove himself as well. Likewise, it was beneficial that the prince usually only prescribed 'what' he should compose, while the 'how' was left to him almost entirely. It was irksome to Haydn that during his three decades in the service of the Esterházys, he had to compose more in some forms than he would have liked to. In the mid-sixties, these were compositions for the baryton, the instrument that the prince himself played, and from 1770, operas for special occasions. The many mechanical tasks which these involved robbed Haydn of time and energy which he would have preferred to devote to his own work. In the two major forms of instrumental music, the string quartet and the symphony, the composition of a series indubitably benefited his musical development.

Living in the country, which at times appeared to Haydn as a distinct drawback, even as a captivity, did not mean that he was cut off from the musical life of Europe. His encounters with the music of C. P. E. Bach as well as with the works of other contemporary composers which Haydn performed with his ensemble left their mark on his steadily changing style. Even during his first ten years as a conductor, occasionally he composed for 'Europe' not only for Prince Esterházy, and from the beginning of the seventies, he did so with increasing frequency. However, there was one serious disadvantage: he was unable to experience himself the effect of his works in France, Spain, England and Germany. He received only reports of the successes, and sometimes also of the failures of his music. It was as if he were working for an imaginary audience; with gradual but constant innovations of style, increasing the scope of his ambitions, increasingly modern, adapting himself, perhaps unconsciously, to the tastes of an unknown and invisible audience. He was driven by his restlessness. He did not adopt a proved routine, like so many of his gifted contemporaries, who in their younger years were carried away by the stream of musical life in Paris, London or other musical centres, and who soon commanded 'impressive', 'agreeable' and 'successful' tricks, and who repeated them incessantly until both their talents and their music became entirely platitudinous. But when Haydn finally reached a wider world after his uninterrupted search for something new, which had lasted thirty-odd years, and came to know another country and another people in England, when he finally faced the audience for which he had composed for many years, he only needed to perfect the timbre of his music by a very little. Enriched by new inspiration, he could go even one step further, beyond the musical style which he himself had developed and which in the meantime had become a world-wide language; so that he was able to inaugurate a new epoch in music.

The often difficult thirty years that Haydn spent almost in the one place, in a prince's establishment in Austria–Hungary, also influenced his artistic development in other no less important respects. Most of Haydn's contemporaries from Austria, Bohemia or other countries, who spent long years abroad, acquired a 'cosmopolitan' language of music, which was blended from the style of Italian musicians who were flooding the whole of Europe, from the music practised in the country where they lived, and from recollections of their native tunes. The majority of them lost their individuality, but more significantly, lost any national character in their music. Haydn, on the other hand, remained the greatest 'national' composer of his time, raising the music of the Austrian people to the highest degree of art. It is, however, worth noting that this 'national' music was pervaded by elements of Hungarian, Croatian and Bohemian folk music and of the 'alla turca' style. However, the Austrian state of the eighteenth century represented the same conglomeration of diverse national elements.

Three decades in the service of the Princes Esterházy, which stimulated Haydn to experiment and to search responsibly for a representative style, afforded him both the opportunities, and, to a large extent, the peace to compose. This 'peace' produced in some of his contemporaries (to mention only Michael Haydn in Salzburg, and Dittersdorf in Johannisberg, who belonged to his narrower circle) a certain dullness, because their creative initiative was replaced by routine. It is evidence of Haydn's human and artistic greatness that with his relatively sparse education and without fully perceiving the spiritual and social development of Europe, he was nevertheless able to interpret burning contemporary issues. From 1760 until his last compositions he was almost always 'modern' and experimental; and this is apparent both in the form and style of his works, as well as in their content.

His development falls into three sharply distinguished periods; these were not simply stages of a stylistic development, which can be broken up readily into more detailed subdivisions of shorter stages. The first great period of his career began when he was appointed conductor to Prince Esterházy. This period reached its peak around 1772–3, by which time Haydn had freed himself from the decorative superficiality of rococo music-making, from the uninspired language of agreeable divertissements; he had found himself and had learned to compose without commonplaces. For the first time music was able to reflect the sentiments and thoughts of the new musical audience, the bourgeoisie. New forms corresponded to the new musical content: through the different types of instrumental music, an entirely new rhythmical structure developed. Through this enrichment of musical forms, by the revival of polyphony and the bold combination of popular elements with artistic forms, music again perfectly expressed the *zeitgeist*, for the first time since Bach and Handel. This highpoint of the years 1772–3 is frequently associated with the *Sturm und Drang* period of German literature, and it is frequently called the 'romantic crisis' of Haydn. But in the light of recent research, not only this literary parallel, but the whole concept of a 'crisis' seems arguable. This style was the culmination of Haydn's stylistic experiments, especially in the two genres whose forms were established by Haydn himself: the string quartet and the symphony.

Though unrelated to the romantic crisis, this idiom was extremely individual. Haydn had moved so far from the conventions of contemporary musical forms that, being blessed with a sense of realism, he drew back before long from this extremist path. His hesitant period, his apparent decline after 1775, was followed from 1780 onwards by the second important period of Haydn's art. Haydn's new objectives were to encompass the enlarged knowledge of the universe, to reach an audience which grew by leaps and bounds, to extend the range of thought that could be expressed through music, and to formulate for this an unequivocal expression, a style of universal appeal, and to establish its rules. In this period Haydn's style became truly 'classical', a model for a universal, European style of music that developed into a 'common language'. The forms of his musical language gradually ceased to belong to him alone. He could hear again in the works of his contemporaries his own analytical thematic technique, the striking ideas of his rondos and pseudo-reprises, his suggestive instrumentation, and the numerous variations of his musical genre-pictures. His greatest contemporary, Mozart, carried his achievements even further, with such brilliance that Haydn in turn learnt from Mozart. The last period of Haydn's work was closely connected with his experiences on his journeys to England. Personal contact with western European audiences had some effect on his style. After experiencing the response of his audience so directly, he felt it necessary to retouch his musical technique here and there. Even more important, he recognized changes in the character of his audience and in social relationships. He had to abandon many of the illusions which he had embodied in his music. After he left Austria, a country which hardly kept abreast of world progress, he perceived through the commonplace events of daily life the crisis of the epoch, the irresolvable disharmony of cities which were split into hostile strata, and the tottering of an entire world order. 'Classical' art, depending on a uniform picture of the world, on a language valid for and understood by everyone, proved to be an illusion. Haydn probably never entirely grasped this, or considered its effects on the social order, and he certainly never formulated it in so many words, but he expressed an unconscious recognition in his late works. For once, his two oratorios were an attempt to comprehend a different community of people, a 'nation' in today's sense of the word. With an intensity previously unknown to him, he expressed the essential traits common to the Austrian peasant, the townsman and the nobleman. In his latest instrumental works, where, in spite of his conscious endeavours, he finally abandoned the classical form, he gave free play to new, restless, subjective and yet widely felt sentiments, which later became typical of romantic art. In his sixties, he strove for the extension of harmonies, the discovery of the sound of the romantic song, the representation of restlessness and spiritual stress through a 'micro-thematic' work, which was carried on by Beethoven, Schubert and later composers. But his era still failed to comprehend this type of music.

It was only in his music that this simple, modest man was revealed as one of the greatest, boldest and most farsighted spirits of his time. His compositions, which were created without apparent internal strife, in manuscripts written clearly and carefully, almost without preliminary drafts or sketches, are the key to his personality. They assure his place among the most important innovators in the history of music, among the few able to express the truest and deepest aspects of the human soul.

PICTURES

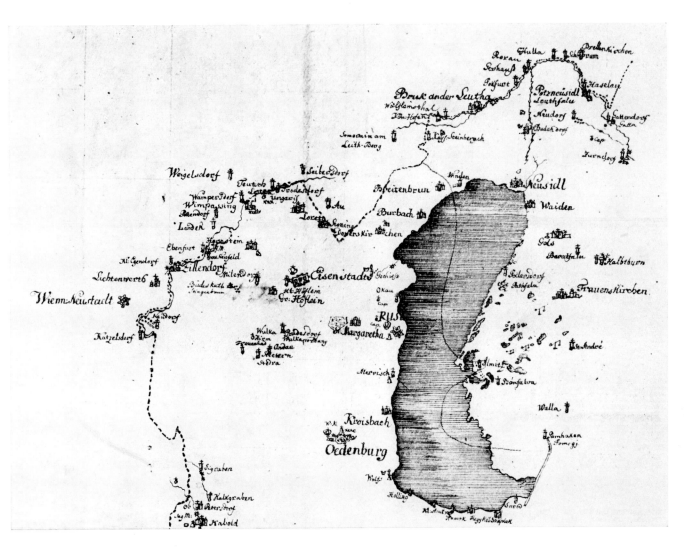

1 HUNGARIAN MAP,
DATING FROM 1730
THE VILLAGE WHERE
HAYDN WAS BORN,
ROHRAU (SPELT RORAU),
IS IN THE TOP
RIGHTHAND CORNER

The ancestors of Joseph Haydn lived in the gentle, hilly country between Lake Fertő and the Danube, a borderland inhabited by both Austrians and Hungarians. South Germans and Croatians settled in the devastated country in the late seventeenth and early eighteenth centuries after the Turks had been driven out, and made the region even more colourful with their dialects and customs and their unusual folklore. In this melting-pot of nationalities Haydn remained Austrian. He never learned to speak either Hungarian or Croatian.

*Joseph Haydn was born on March 31, 1732, at Rohrau, a village in Lower Austria, in the district Unter Wiener Wald near the Hungarian border, not far from the town of Bruck an der Leitha.* (Griesinger)

THE
FAMILY HOUSE
IN ROHRAU

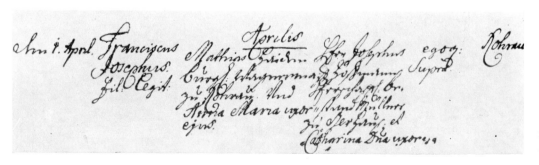

His ancestors were simple peasants and artisans, who worked hard and lived modestly. Twelve children were born from the first marriage of his father, the cartwright Mathias Haydn, with Anna Maria Koller. Franz Joseph was the second. He was the eldest of the three brothers who survived infancy.

*Ansicht des Schlosses Rohrau.*      *Vue du château de Rohrau.*

4 THE CASTLE OF ROHRAU

*The father, an ordinary cartwright and justice of the peace in Rohrau, was married to a woman who had been in service as a cook with the gentry of the place...* (Dies)
*In his youth the father journeyed about following the custom of his trade, and reached Frankfurt am Main, where he learned to play the harp a little and, because he liked to sing, to accompany himself on the harp as well as he could. Afterwards, when he was married, he kept the habit of singing, a little to amuse himself. All the children had to join in his concerts, to learn the songs, and to develop their singing voice. When his father sang, Joseph, at the age of five, used to accompany him as children will by playing with a stick on a piece of wood, which his childish powers of imagination transformed into a violin.* (Dies)

*My late father was a wheelwright by profession, and served Count Harrach, a great lover of music by nature. He [my father] played the harp without knowing a note of music, and as a boy of five, I correctly sang all his simple little pieces; this induced my father to entrust me to the care of my relative, the schoolmaster in Haimburg, in order that I might learn the rudiments of music and the other juvenile acquirements.* (Haydn)

*One day the headmaster from the neighbouring town of Hainburg, a distant relative of the
Haydn family, came to Rohrau. Meister Mathias and his wife gave their usual little concert,
and five-year-old Joseph sat near his parents and sawed at his left arm with a stick, as if
he were accompanying on the violin. It astonished the schoolteacher that the boy observed
the time so correctly. He inferred from this a natural talent for music and advised the parents
to send their Sepperl (an Austrian diminutive for Joseph) to Hainburg so that he might
be set to the acquisition of an art that in time would unfailingly open to him the prospect 'of
becoming a clergyman'. The parents, ardent admirers of the clergy, joyfully seized this
proposal, and in his sixth year, Joseph Haydn went to the headmaster in Hainburg. Here
he received instruction in reading and writing, in catechism, in singing, and in almost all
wind and string instruments, even in the timpani. 'I shall owe it to this man even in my
grave,' Haydn oftentimes said, 'that he set me to so many different things, although I received in the process more thrashings than food.'* (Griesinger)

*Almighty God (to Whom alone I owe the most profound gratitude) endowed me, especially
in music, with such proficiency that even in my sixth year I was able to sing some masses
in the choir-loft, and to play a little on the harpsichord and violin.* (Haydn)

6 THE PANORAMA OF HAINBURG ON THE DANUBE, WHERE HAYDN'S GRANDPARENTS AND GREAT-GRANDPARENTS LIVED

# THE FIRST APPRENTICESHIP: HAINBURG

7 THE 'ROMAN TOWER' IN HAINBURG

Die Schlag. Brücke                    Le pont du Leopoldstadt

C P S G M                    Bey Artaria & comp

In 1740 at the age of eight Joseph Haydn came to know Vienna, the capital which had become the meeting place of the most important ideas from both East and West.

EARLY YEARS
IN VIENNA

*Haydn, who even then wore a wig for the sake of cleanliness, had been some three years in Hainburg when the Court Kapellmeister Reutter, of Vienna, director of music at St. Stephen's Cathedral, visited his friend the dean in Hainburg. Reutter told the dean that his older choirboys, whose voices were beginning to break, would be useless to him, and that he had to replace them with younger subjects. The dean proposed the eight-year-old Haydn, and he and the schoolmaster were called at once. The poorly nourished Sepperl cast longing glances at the cherries that were sitting on the dean's table. Reutter tossed a few handfuls into his hat, and seemed well pleased with the Latin and Italian strophes that Haydn had to sing. 'Can you also make a trill?' asked Reutter. 'No,' said Haydn, 'for not even my cousin can do that.' This answer greatly embarrassed the schoolteacher, and Reutter laughed uproariously. He demonstrated the mechanical principle of trilling, Haydn imitated him, and at the third attempt succeeded. 'You shall stay with me,' said Reutter. The departure from Hainburg soon followed, and Haydn came as a pupil to the Choir School at St. Stephen's Cathedral in Vienna, where he stayed until his sixteenth year. (Griesinger)*

6

9 THE PALACE OF
SCHÖNBRUNN, THE
IMPERIAL RESIDENCE,
WHICH JOSEPH HAYDN
OCCASIONALLY PASSED BY
DURING HIS YEARS AS
A CHOIR-BOY

10 THE CORONATION
PROCESSION OF MARIA
THERESA ALONG THE
GRABEN, ONE OF
VIENNA'S SPLENDID
SQUARES (1740)

11 View of Vienna,
from the Belvedere,

AROUND 1760, BY
BERNARDO BELLOTTO

9

*pag. 47*

*Besides the scant instruction usual at the time in Latin, in religion, in arithmetic and writing, Haydn had in the Choir School very capable instructors on several instruments, and especially in singing. Among the latter were Gegenbauer, a functionary of the Court Chorus, and an elegant tenor, Finsterbusch.* (Griesinger)

13 Johann Joseph Fux
(1660–1741)

He also came to know Mattheson's Der vollkommene Kapellmeister [1739], and Fux's
Gradus ad Parnassum [1725] in German and Latin—a book he still in his old age praised
as a classic and of which he had kept a hard-used copy. (Griesinger)

I admit I had the gift: with this and with much hard work I made great strides. (Haydn)

11

*No instruction in music theory was undertaken in the Choir School, and Haydn remembered
receiving only two lessons in this from the excellent Reutter. But Reutter did encourage him
to make whatever variations he liked on the motets and* Salves *that he had to sing through
in the church, and this practice early led him to ideas of his own which Reutter corrected.*
(Griesinger)

*Joseph was then already busy with composition in his spare time. Reutter surprised him
once just as he had spread out a* Salve regina *in twelve parts on a yard-long sheet of paper.
'Hey! What are you up to there, boy?'—Reutter looked over the long paper, laughed heartily
at the copious sprinkling of* Salves, *still more at the boy's preposterous notion that he could
compose in twelve parts, and added: 'Aren't two voices enough for you, you little blockhead?'*
(Dies)

*Reutter was so captivated by the boy's talents that he declared to his father that even if he
had twelve sons, he would take care of them all. The father saw himself freed of a great
burden by this offer, consented to it, and some five years after dedicated Joseph's brother
Michael and still later Johann to the musical muse. Both were taken on as choirboys, and,
ot Joseph's unending joy, both brothers were turned over to him to be trained.* (Dies)

15 THE 'CHOIR HOUSE'
AT THE WEST FRONT
OF ST. STEPHEN'S
CATHEDRAL

In the immediate vicinity of St. Stephen's Cathedral, between a four-storey block of flats and the Magdalen Chapel, stood the house of the choir-master, Reutter. Here lived the six choir-boys, one of whom was Joseph Haydn. Five years later, in the autumn of 1745, his brother Michael joined him there.

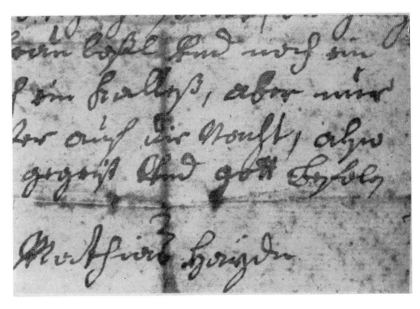

16 THE SIGNATURE OF
MATHIAS HAYDN ON
A LETTER TO HIS SONS

*Since Haydn because of his cracked voice was unfit to be a choirboy any longer and thus had no further monetary value for Kapellmeister Reutter, the latter found it only fair to discharge him. A piece of mischief on his own part hastened Haydn's dismissal. One of the other choirboys, contrary to the usual costume of a choirboy at that time, wore his long hair in a pigtail. Haydn, out of sheer mischief, cut it off for him! Reutter called him to account and sentenced him to a caning on the palm of the hand. The moment of punishment arrived. Haydn sought every means to escape it, and ended up declaring that he would rather not be a choirboy any more and would leave immediately, if he would not be punished. 'That won't work!' Reutter retorted. 'First you'll be caned, and then get out!' (Dies)*

Prospekt von Mariazell
in Obersteyermark

Vue de Mariazell
en Styrie Superieure

18 THE CHURCH AT
MARIAZELL, A PLACE OF
PILGRIMAGE

*Until my eighteenth year I sang soprano with great success, not only at St. Stephen's but also at the Court. Finally I lost my voice, and then had to eke out a wretched existence for eight whole years, by teaching young pupils (many geniuses are ruined by their having to earn their daily bread, because they have no time to study): I experienced this, too, and would have never learnt what little I did, had I not, in my zeal for composition, composed well into the night . . .* (Haydn)

*Soon after his departure from the Choir School Haydn made a pilgrimage to Mariazell. He had in his pocket several motets of his own composition and asked the* Regens chori *there for permission to take them into the church and sing them. This request was denied him; but to achieve his purpose of gaining himself a hearing, he had recourse to trickery on the following day. He placed himself in the choir behind the boy who had the alto part to sing, and offered him a coin [Siebzehner] to give up his place to him. The boy did not dare to make the bargain for fear of the director, so then Haydn reached quickly over the boy's head, seized the music on the desk, and sang to everybody's satisfaction. The* Regens chori *got together a collection of sixteen gulden and sent the hopeful youth back to Vienna with it.* (Griesinger)

15

Aufscht des Kohlmarkts       Vue du Kohlmarkt.

19 THE 'OLD
MICHAELERHAUS' IN
VIENNA, NEAR THE
HOFBURG

*...He could not expect the least support from his poor parents, and so had to try to make his own way by his talent alone. In Vienna he moved into a wretched little attic room without a stove (in the house at No. 1220 in the Michaelerplatz), in which he was scarcely sheltered from the rain.* (Griesinger)

16

20 THE CHURCH OF
THE BROTHERS OF MERCY,
IN THE LEOPOLDSTADT

*Haydn also in this period was first violinist [Vorspieler] for the Brothers of Mercy in the Leopoldstadt, at sixty gulden a year. Here he had to be in the church at eight o'clock in the morning on Sundays and feast days. At ten o'clock he played the organ in the chapel of Count Haugwitz, and at eleven o'clock he sang at St. Stephen's. He was paid seventeen kreutzers for each service. (Griesinger)*

Author und Berühmter Comicus unter den Nähmen Bernardon.
Dem Selben gewidmet von seinen

21 JOSEPH FELIX KURZ
(WHOSE STAGE NAME
WAS BERNARDON;
1717–1784), ONE OF THE
BEST KNOWN FIGURES
OF THE VIENNESE
THEATRE IN HIS TIME,
THE EMBODIMENT OF
THE 'HANSWURST' STYLE

*In the evenings, Haydn oftentimes went out serenading with his musical comrades, when one of his compositions was usually played . . .* (Griesinger)

*Once he went to serenade the wife of [Johann Joseph Felix] Kurz, a comic actor very popular at the time and usually called Bernardon. Kurz came into the street and asked for the composer of the music just played. Hardly had Haydn, who was about nineteen years old, identified himself when Kurz urged him strongly to compose an opera for him. Haydn pleaded his youth in vain; Kurz encouraged him, and Haydn actually composed the opera,* Der krumme Teufel [The Crooked Devil], *a satire on the lame theatre director Affligio, on whose account it was forbidden after the third performance. Haydn liked to linger over the story of composing this opera, because it reminded him of Bernardon's many comic traits. Harlequin ran away from the waves in* Der krumme Teufel. *To illustrate this Bernardon lay down at full length over several chairs and imitated all the movements of a swimmer. 'See how I swim! See how I swim!' Kurz called out to Haydn who was sitting at the clavier and who at once, to the poet's great satisfaction, fell into six-eight time.* (Griesinger)

18

A. Die Schotten-Kirche. B. Hartigisches Gebäude. A. L'Eglise des Benedictins Ecossois. B. Hôtel de Harrach.
D. Lambergisches. C. Hôtel de Thaun. D. Hôtel de Lamberg.

Der Schotten Platz.     La Place des Ecossois.

22 A 'HANSWURST' STAGE
ON THE FREYUNG.
ON THE LEFT, THE
HARRACH FAMILY'S
VIENNA PALACE

23–24 THE TITLE-PAGE
AND COLOPHON OF THE
LIBRETTO OF THE SECOND
COMIC OPERA WRITTEN
BY HAYDN IN
COLLABORATION WITH
BERNARDON
(HOBOKEN XXIXB: 1)

Der neue

Krumme Teufel.

Eine

OPERA-COMIQUE

von zwey Aufzügen;

Nebst einer

Kinder-Pantomime,

Betitult:

ARLEQUIN

Der neue Abgott Ram

in America.

Alles componiret

Von Joseph Kurz.

CHORUS.

Alle. { Wahre Lieb sucht alle Gänge,
{ Alle Vortheil, alle List,
{ Bis der Gegner in die Länge,
{ Endlich doch betrogen ist.

Bernardon.
Gleich und gleich gehört zusammen.

Fiametta.
Gleich, und gleich liebt jedermann,
O das sind die schönsten Flammen,
Die die Tugend zündet an.

Alle. { Wahre Lieb sucht alle Gänge,
{ Alle Vortheil, alle List,
{ Biß der Gegner in die Länge,
{ Endlich doch betrogen ist.

ENDE.

NB. die Musique sowohl von der Opera-Comique,
als auch der Pantomime ist componiret

Von

Herrn Joseph Heyden.

19

P. METASTASIVS
ROMANVS.

25 PIETRO METASTASIO
(1698–1782), THE MOST
FAMOUS LIBRETTIST
OF HIS TIME, WHO,
AFTER 1730, ALSO LIVED IN
THE 'OLD MICHAELERHAUS'

*. . . I wrote diligently, but not quite correctly, until at last I had the good fortune to learn the true fundamentals of composition from the celebrated Herr Porpora (who was at that time in Vienna).* (Haydn)

*In the same house in which Joseph Haydn was quartered dwelt also the celebrated poet Metastasio. The latter was educating a Fräulein Martinez. Haydn gave her lessons in singing and clavier playing and received in return free board for three years. Through Metastasio Haydn also learned to know the now aged Kapellmeister Porpora. Porpora gave the mistress of Correr, the Venetian ambassador, lessons in singing, and because Porpora was too grand and too fond of his ease to accompany on the pianoforte himself, he entrusted this business to our Giuseppe. 'There was no lack of* Asino, Coglione, Birbante *[ass, cullion, rascal], and pokes in the ribs, but I put up with it all, for I profited greatly with Porpora in singing, in composition, and in the Italian language.' Correr travelled in summer with the lady to the then much frequented baths at Mannersdorf, not far from Bruck. Porpora went there too in order to continue the lessons, and he took Haydn with him . . . Here he sometimes had to accompany on the clavier for Porpora at a Prince von Hildburghausen's, in the presence of Gluck, Wagenseil, and other celebrated masters, and the approval of such connoisseurs served as a special encouragement to him.* (Griesinger)

*De l'art d'aller au cœur par des accords touchants*
*Nul autre mieux que lui n'a montré la puissance,*
*Et de tous ses rivaux c'est le seul dont les chants*
*Ayent charmé son pays, l'Italie et la France.*

27 Christoph Willibald
Gluck (1714–1787)

28 Carl Philipp
Emanuel Bach
(1714–1788)

*About this time Haydn came upon the first six sonatas of
Emanuel Bach. 'I did not come away from my clavier till I
had played through them, and whoever knows me thoroughly
must discover that I owe a great deal to Emanuel Bach, that
I understood him and have studied him diligently. Emanuel
Bach once made me a compliment on this score himself.'
...So I made inquiry of Haydn whether he had known Sammartini's works in his youth, and what he thought of this
composer. Haydn answered me that he had heard Sammartini's music before that time, but had never valued it 'because
Sammartini was a scribbler [Schmierer].' (Griesinger)*

21

*A Baron Fürnberg had a palace in Weinzierl, several stages [about fifty miles] from Vienna, and he invited from time to time his pastor, his manager, Haydn, and Albrechtsberger (a brother of the celebrated contrapuntist, who played the violoncello) in order to have a little music. Fürnberg requested Haydn to compose something that could be performed by these four amateurs. Haydn, then eighteen years old, took up this proposal, and so originated his first quartet which, immediately it appeared, received such general approval that Haydn took courage to work further in this form.* (Griesinger)

29 WEINZIERL NEAR WIESELBURG IN LOWER AUSTRIA, THE ESTATE OF KARL JOSEPH, BARON VON FÜRNBERG

30 A CONTEMPORARY COPY OF THE FIRST SYMPHONY (HOBOKEN I: 1, AROUND 1759), FROM THE FORMER FÜRNBERG ARCHIVES

31 THE FIRST MOVEMENT OF HAYDN'S FIRST SYMPHONY, WHICH BEGINS WITH A 'MANNHEIM CRESCENDO' (HOBOKEN I: 1)

22

32 MANUSCRIPT OF THE
FIRST BARS OF THE ORGAN
CONCERTO IN C MAJOR
COMPOSED IN 1756
(HOBOKEN XVIII: 1)

Haydn's first compositions of 'artistic music' (i.e. those not meant for the popular stage or for serenades) whose manuscripts have survived, purposely avoided any resemblance to folk songs and 'Gassenhauers'. Following in the style of Reutter, Wagenseil and other recognized Viennese masters, they conformed to the taste of knowledgeable, educated noblemen. As a result of their distinction, Haydn, in his twenty-seventh year, was employed by Count Morzin, who lived alternately in Vienna and on his Bohemian estate at Lukavec, as director of his orchestra.

*In the year 1759 Haydn was appointed in Vienna to be music director to Count Morzin with a salary of two hundred gulden, free room, and board at the staff table. Here he enjoyed at last the good fortune of a care-free existence; it suited him thoroughly. The winter was spent in Vienna and the summer in Bohemia, in the vicinity of Pilsen. (Griesinger)*

*My good mother ... who was always solicitous for my well-being, was no longer among the living; but my father lived long enough to rejoice at seeing me as a Kapellmeister. (Haydn)*

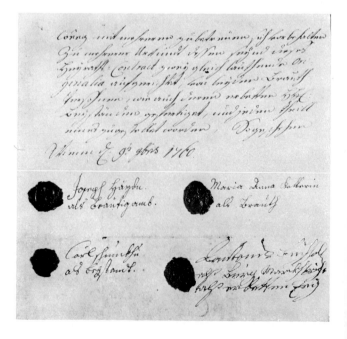

33 (Left) The certificate
of the marriage
performed in
St. Stephen's
Cathedral

34 (Right) The high
altar of St. Stephen's
Cathedral

35 Last page of the
marriage certificate
at the Registrar's

*Haydn had oftentimes received help in the house of a hairdresser in Vienna (in the Landstrasse) named Keller; he also gave music lessons to the eldest daughter, and his preference for her grew with closer acquaintance. But she entered a convent, and Haydn then decided, since his future was somewhat secured by a fixed salary and the hairdresser, to whom he felt grateful, kept urging it, that he would marry the second daughter. Haydn had no children by this marriage. 'My wife was unable to bear children, and I was therefore less indifferent to the charms of other ladies.' His choice did not turn out very well in general, for his wife was of a domineering, unfriendly character. He had to be careful to conceal his income from her, because she loved to spend, was bigoted on the subject, was continually inviting the clergy to dinner, had many masses said, and was freer with charitable contributions than her situation warranted. Once, when I was obliged to inquire of Haydn how a favour he had shown and for which he would take nothing, could be repaid to his wife, he answered me: 'She does not deserve anything, and it is all the same to her if her husband is a shoemaker or an artist.' (Griesinger)*

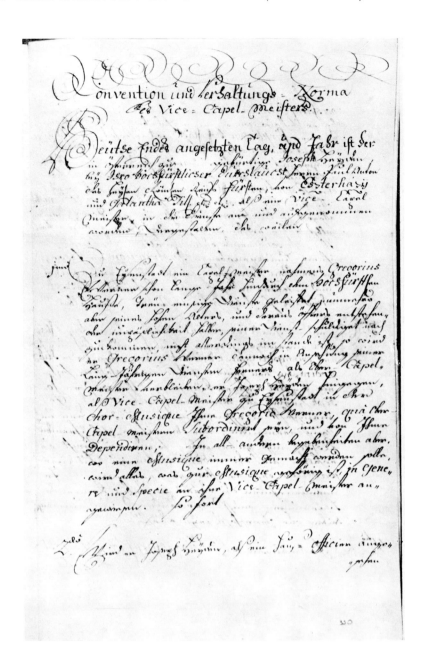

*Agreement and conditions of conduct for a Vice-Kapellmeister*
*On the day and in the year given at the foot of this contract, Joseph Heyden, born in Austria (Rohrau) has been employed as Vice-Kapellmeister in the service of His Serene Highness Paul Anton, Prince of The Holy Roman Empire Eszterházy and Galantha Tit. etc. etc., upon the following terms:*
*1st. For many years there has been in Eysenstadt a Kapellmeister Gregorius Werner, who has rendered faithful service to the princely house, but on account of his great age and the incapacity often resulting therefrom can no longer fulfil his duties, he, Gregorius Werner, in consideration of his services of many years will remain head Kapellmeister, and the aforementioned Joseph Heyden will be Vice-Kapellmeister in Eysenstadt, subordinate to and answering to Gregorio Werner in choir music; but in all other matters, where music has to be made, everything pertaining to music will at once become responsibility in genere and specie of the Vice-Kapellmeister.*
*2nd. Joseph Heyden will be considered an officer of the house. Therefore, His Serene Highness*

At the time when Joseph Haydn entered his employment, the baroque town of Eisenstadt (Kismarton), on the western shore of Lake Fertő, was the permanent residence of the Princes Esterházy.

37 VIEW OF EISENSTADT (KISMARTON)

38 THE ESTERHÁZY PALACE AT EISENSTADT

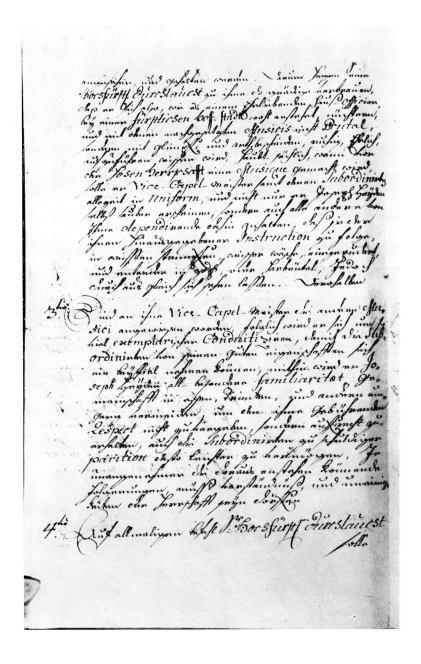

shows him the gracious trust that he will, as befits an honest house officer in a princely
court, behave soberly and, to the musicians directed by him, not brutishly but gently,
modestly, calmly and honestly, especially when music is to be made in front of His Highness,
and not only shall the Vice-Kapellmeister Joseph Heyden together with his subordinates,
appear at all times clean and in livery, but he will also see that all those answering to him
follow the instructions given to them and appear in white stockings, white shirt, powdered,
and pig-tails, dressed alike. Therefore

3rd. All musicians are subordinated to the Vice-Kapellmeister, consequently he will behave
himself in an exemplary manner, so that his subordinates can follow the example of his
good qualities; he will avoid any undue familiarity in eating and drinking or otherwise in
his relations with them, lest he should lose the respect due to him, but will maintain his
demeanour in such a way as to ensure that his subordinates obey him. Consequences that
could arise from exaggerated familiarity should not lead to misunderstandings and quarrels.

4th. At the command of His Serene Highness the Vice-Kapellmeister is liable to compose

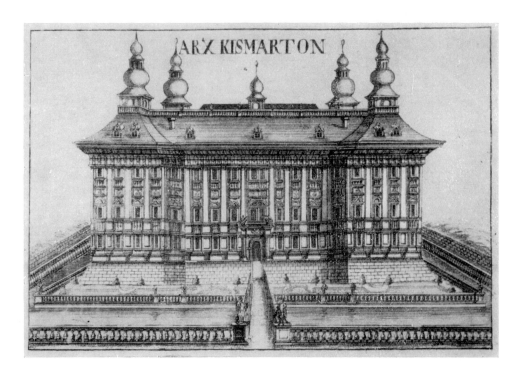

ARX KISMARTON

40 The Palace in
Eisenstadt in the
form which the
poet and
composer Palatine Paul
Esterházy (1635–1713)
gave it through
commissioning its
rebuilding by the
Italian architect
Carlone after 1660

41 Plan dated 1760
for the reconstruction
of the park at
Eisenstadt in the
spirit of French
gardens

such music as His Serene Highness may require of him, such compositions are not to be
communicated to any person, nor copied, but remain the property of His Serene Highness,
and without the knowledge and permission of His Serene Highness, he is not to compose for
any person.

5th. Joseph Heyden shall appear daily (whether in Vienna or on the estate) in the morning
and in the afternoon in the ante-chamber and will be announced and will await the decision
of His Serene Highness whether there should be music, and after having received the order,
will inform the other musicians, and not only appear himself punctually at the appointed
time but also ensure that the rest appear, and should a musician either come late for the
music or even be absent, he will take his name.

6th. Should, regrettably, quarrels or complaints occur among the musicians, the Vice-Kapellmeister shall attempt in accordance with the circumstances to settle them, so that His
Grace will not be importuned with trifling matters; but should a more important incident
occur that he, Joseph Heyden, cannot himself settle by mediation, he shall faithfully repor
it to His Serene Highness.

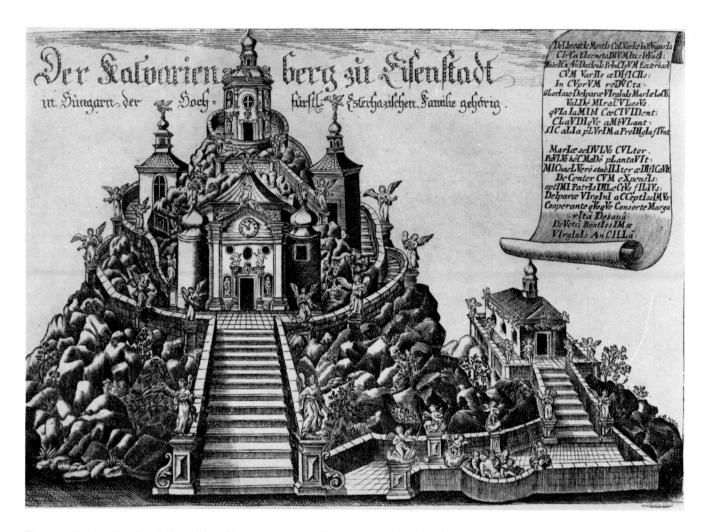

From 1727 to his death in 1766, Gregor Joseph Werner was the leading director of the prince's musical ensemble at Eisenstadt. Although he had no outstanding talents, he was a highly educated and creative composer. His musical style, refreshed by popular elements, rests on baroque traditions (primarily, on the music of J. J. Fux). This style, which sounded obsolete by the middle of the century, was fundamentally challenged by Joseph Haydn.

43 THE BERGKIRCHE IN EISENSTADT

44 A PAGE FROM THE MANUSCRIPT OF WERNER'S ORATORIO 'DEBORAH', FIRST PERFORMED IN 1760

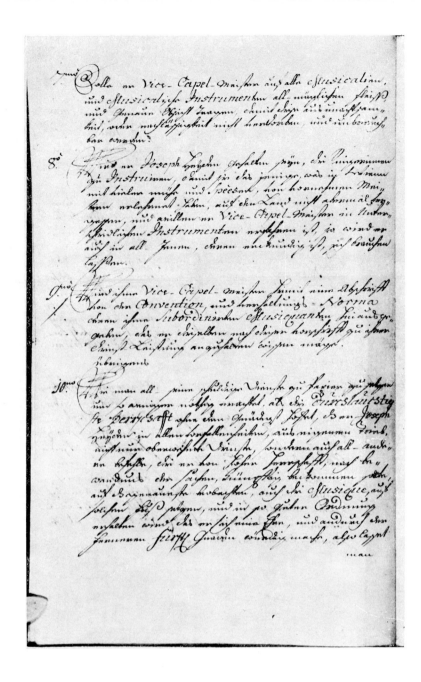

7th. The Vice-Kapellmeister shall survey and take care of all musical instruments, so that they should not be spoiled or made unusable through inattention or negligence.

8th. Joseph Heyden is obliged to instruct the female singers, so that they should not forget in the country what they have learnt in Vienna from distinguished masters at great trouble and expense, and since the Vice-Kapellmeister has experience of various instruments, he will allow himself to be employed in playing all those instruments with which he is acquainted.

9th. The Vice-Kapellmeister will receive herewith a copy of the convention and norms of behaviour of his subordinate musicians, so that he will know how to make them behave in service, in accordance with these regulations.

10th. As it is not considered necessary to commit to paper all the services that he is obliged to perform, seeing that His Serene Highness graciously hopes that Joseph Heyden will in all matters spontaneously carry out not only the above-mentioned services, but also all other orders of His Grace that he may receive in future, and also maintain the music in good

With this contract began for Haydn three decades of service. At first, this was a 'service' in the feudal meaning of the word. Haydn became an 'employee' of the richest aristocratic family in Hungary, a link in the conventional line of subordination. His first princely lord, Paul Anton, contrary to the family tradition, had received only a German and a French education instead of being brought up as a Hungarian. Highly educated, a friend of all the arts, he played the violin and the violoncello. When in Italy in 1750 as imperial envoy, he came to know the operatic life of Rome and Naples. Deeply impressed, he established a rich collection of music to raise the standard of musical life at his residence. In 1759 he sent the violinist Luigi Tomasini and the tenor Carl Friberth on a study tour of Italy. In the conservatory of the palace park, a theatre was established. The prince died in March 1762, shortly before its opening.

*Haydn's father thus had the pleasure of seeing his son in the uniform of that family, blue, trimmed with gold, and of hearing from the Prince many eulogies of the talent of his son. A short time after this visit, a wood pile fell on Meister Mathias while he was at work. He suffered broken ribs and died soon thereafter. (Griesinger)*

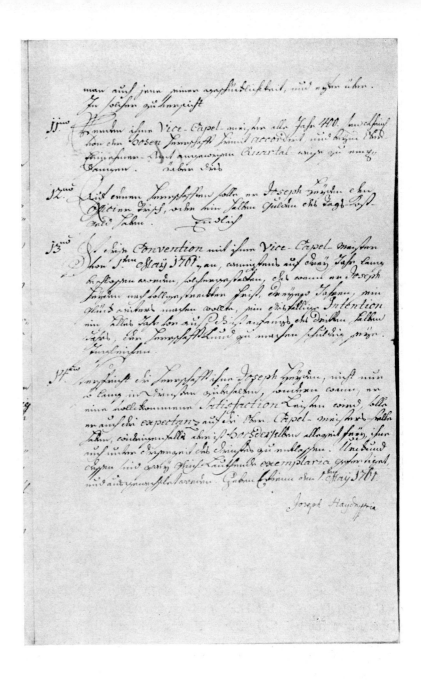

order so that he will become worthy of respect and of princely favour, all these shall be left to his skill and industry. In confidence of this

11th. The Vice-Kapellmeister will be accorded by His Lordship four hundred guilder annually, payment to be made quarterly by the Chief Cashier. In addition to this

12th. Joseph Heyden shall receive his meals at the officers' table or half a guilder for board daily. Finally,

13th. This convention was concluded on the 1st May, 1761 with the Vice-Kapellmeister for at least three years, provided that if Joseph Heyden wishes to continue in this honour after having served for three years, he must announce his intention to His Lordship six months in advance, that is at the beginning of the third year. Similarly

14th. His Lordship promises not only to keep Joseph Heyden in his service for the agreed period, but if he gives full satisfaction, he may expect the position of Principal Kapellmeister; should the contrary be the case however, His Serene Highness is free at any time to dismiss him from his service. Witness to which two identical copies have been prepared and exchanged. Vienna, 1st May, 1761.

*Joseph Haydn mppria*

# PRINCE NIKOLAUS
## 'THE MAGNIFICENT'

48 (LEFT) THE FIRST
PRINCE NIKOLAUS
ESTERHÁZY 'THE
MAGNIFICENT' (1714–1790)

49 (RIGHT) THE ADDRESS
FROM ONE OF HAYDN'S
PETITIONS TO THE PRINCE.
('SERENE HIGHNESS AND
NOBLE PRINCE OF
THE HOLY ROMAN
EMPIRE, GRACIOUS AND
DREAD LORD!')

After the inaugural celebrations on the 17th May, 1762, Prince Nicolaus 'the Magnificent' entered into his brother's heritage. He was forty-eight years old, full of ideas and plans. From the point of view of Hungarian national politics, he may be considered a reactionary aristocrat, faithful to the Emperor, who placed neither his time nor his energy nor his immeasurable wealth at the service of Hungarian nationalism, but gave his whole attention to the well-being of his own 'realm'. And yet, the 'Esterházy Fairyland', with its buildings on the grand scale, its theatre and not least its music directed by Haydn, became an important chapter in Hungary's cultural history.

*Serene Highness and Noble Prince of the Holy Roman Empire, Gracious and Dread Lord!*
*I have received with every submissive and dutiful respect Your Illustrious and Serene Highness' letter..., and I see from it that Your Highness has taken it very amiss that I protested against the detention of the* flauto traverso *player Frantz Sigl to Herr von Rahier... But we could not get anywhere with the administrator, and I even had to put up with his slamming the door in my face, he... threatened everyone with detention... I myself told the administrator to complain to Your Serene and Illustrious Highness if he felt his own person to have been insulted, but I was given the answer that the administrator is his own judge and will meet out the punishment himself. Everyone... hopes that Your Serene and Gracious Highness... will graciously put a stop to such a procedure, whereby anyone can be his own judge without differentiating between guilty or not guilty... But moreover Your Serene and Illustrious Highness must yourself remember, in your graciousness, that I cannot serve two masters, and cannot accept the commands of, and subordinate myself to, the administrator, for Your Serene and Illustrious Highness once said to me: come first to me, because I am his master...* (Haydn, Eisenstadt, 9 September, 1765)

34

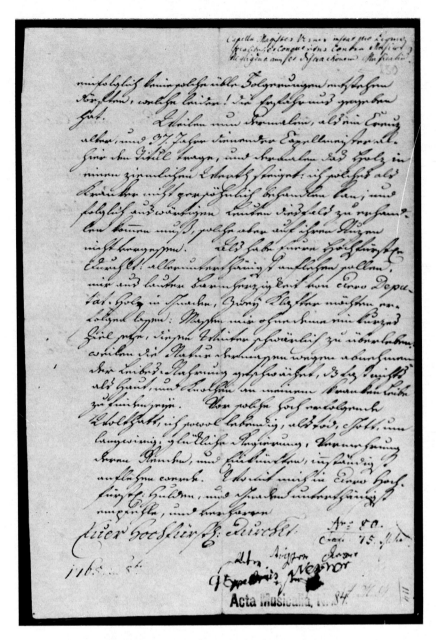

50 LAST PAGE OF G. J.
WERNER'S PETITION (1765)

51 PART OF THE MANUSCRIPT
OF THE BENEDICTUS FROM
HAYDN'S 'MISSA SOLEMNIS'
IN HONOREM B. V. M.,
WITH ORGAN OBBLIGATO
(HOBOKEN XXII: 4)

*Serene Highness and Noble Prince of the Holy Roman Empire. Gracious and Respected Lord!*
*I am compelled to report some wholly unjustified expenses to your Highness, and the complete idleness of the entire musical ensemble, for which the director must bear the chief blame. He turns a blind eye to anything, so long as they call him 'the good Heyden'... But in the meantime the collection of music... could be completely spoilt if a serious command is not given to the reported Heyden, that he should prepare a catalogue at least of those parts which are still there. Further, I must humbly ask Your Serene Highness to issue to him a severe command that he keep strict order among the musicians of the choir and that they in future, all without exception, should appear at services. And since it can be surmised that Heyden will want to clear himself through denials, Your Highness' order should be given that all choir instruments should be examined... this will soon show where the truth lies...*
(Werner, October, 1765)

After the death of Kapellmeister Werner, who had been sick for a long time, on the 3rd March, 1766, Joseph Haydn became Principal Kapellmeister. From then on, church music was also his responsibility.

52 The Prince's baryton with the carved head of a Hungarian 'hajdú'

53 A page of Haydn's so-called 'Entwurf-Katalog' (sketch catalogue, a thematic index) with an entry of his works for the baryton

This stringed instrument belonging to the family of the viola d'amore was held like a violoncello. Under the finger-board there are several strings—here ten—which, in addition to the strings passed over by the bow, could be plucked with the thumb of the left hand.

54 A BARYTON, BELIEVED
TO HAVE BEEN HAYDN'S

*The Prince loved music, and himself played the bary-
ton, which, in his opinion, should be limited to only
one key. Haydn could not be sure about this, because
he had only a very superficial knowledge of the instrument. Still, he believed it must lend itself to several
keys. While Haydn, unbeknown to the Prince, was
conducting an investigation into the nature of the
instrument, he acquired a liking for it and practiced
it late at night, because he had no other time, with a
view toward becoming a good player. To be sure, he
was often interrupted in his nocturnal studies by the
scolding and quarrelling of his wife, but he did not
lose patience and in six months attained his goal.
The Prince still knew nothing. Haydn could resist a
touch of vanity no longer. He played openly in the
presence of the Prince, in several keys, expecting to
earn no end of applause. The Prince, however, was
not at all surprised, took the thing as a matter of
course, and said merely: 'You're supposed to know
these things, Haydn!' 'I understood the Prince perfectly,' Haydn told me, 'and although at first I was
hurt by his indifference, still I owe it to his curt
reminder that I suddenly gave up the intention of
being a good barytonist. I remembered that I had
already gained some note as a Kapellmeister, and
not as a practicing virtuoso, reproached myself for
half a year's neglect of composition, and returned to
it with zeal renewed.' (Dies)*

55 24 TRIOS BY JOSEPH
HAYDN FOR BARYTON,
VIOLA AND BASS, IN THE
SPLENDID LEATHER
BINDING MADE SPECIALLY
FOR THE PRINCE

56 'FATTO A POSTA
NIHIL SINE CAUSA.'
A CHARACTERISTIC
COMMENT ON THE
TITLE-PAGE OF
BARYTON TIRO
(HOBOKEN XI: 109)

*This very moment I received 3 pieces from Hayden, and I am very satisfied with them.
You will therefore see that he gets 12 ducats from the cashier's office in my name; tell him at
the same time to write 6 more pieces similar to those he sent me, and also 2 solo pieces,
and to see that they are forwarded at once. (The Prince to Rahier, 4 January, 1766)*

57 A charming stage
set of antique ruins,
from 1762. (Presumably
by Girolamo Bon,
likewise in the
Prince's service)

Haydn's ensemble performed outside the palace for the first time in the comic opera
*La canterina*, composed in 1766 (Hoboken XXVIII: 2). During the carnival season
of 1767 it was performed in the bishop's residence at Pressburg, in the presence of the
Imperial Family.

58 View of Pressburg

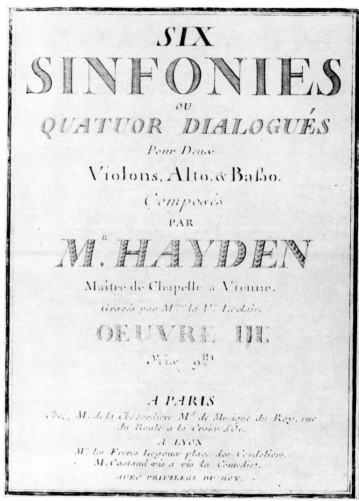

## SUCCESSES ABROAD

The name of Joseph Haydn appeared in print for the first time in 1763, in a catalogue by the publisher Breitkopf. The oldest known Haydn publication appeared in 1764. This was not a breach of contract on Haydn's part. His works—first of all his divertimenti, and his string quartets—were published without his knowledge and without monetary profit to him, and pirated copies reached German and French publishers.

*...Herr Joseph Haydn, the darling of our nation, whose gentle character is marked on each of his pieces. His compositions have beauty, order, clarity, a fine and noble simplicity, which are being sensed even before the listeners are prepared for it. In his divertimento, quartet and trio, there is a pure and clear stream, which is first rippled, then raised into waves, without leaving its bed. He is the originator of the monotonous style of parts in octaves, the pleasing quality of which cannot be denied, when they appear dressed by Haydn. In his symphonies, he is as virile and strong as he is sensitive. In his cantatas, he is charming, conquering, flattering; and in his minuets, natural, jocular, enticing. In short, Haydn is in music what Gellert is in poetry.* ('Of Viennese Taste in Music', *Wiener Diarium*, 18 October, 1766)

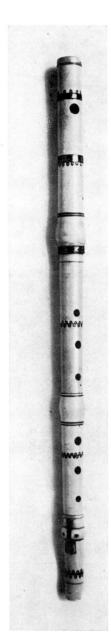

61 THE HOLOGRAPH
OF THE FIRST MOVEMENT
OF THE 'HORN SIGNAL'
SYMPHONY
(HOBOKEN III: 31, 1765)
USING THE DIFFERENT
TIMBRES OF FOUR HORNS,
HAYDN CREATED A
'THEME' WITHOUT
MELODY, RELYING ON
THEIR UNUSUAL,
SUGGESTIVE EFFECT ONLY

*My Prince was content with all my works, I received approval, I could, as head of an orchestra, make experiments, observe what enhanced an effect, and what weakened it, thus improving, adding to, cutting away, and running risks. I was set apart from the world, there was nobody in my vicinity to confuse and annoy me in my course, and so I had to be original.* (Haydn)

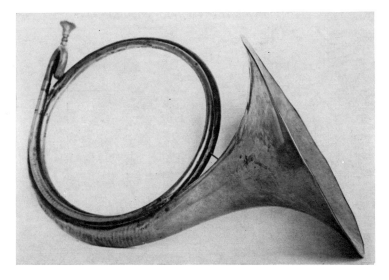

62–63–64 WIND
INSTRUMENTS FROM
HAYDN'S TIME. IN
HAYDN'S EARLIER
SYMPHONIES, AS A RULE
THE STRINGS WERE
COMPLETED BY TWO
OBOI, A FLUTE AND
TWO HORNS

41

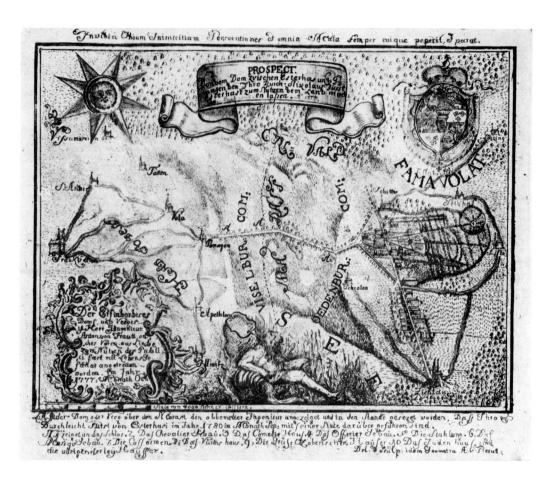

## THE NEW RESIDENCE: ESZTERHÁZA

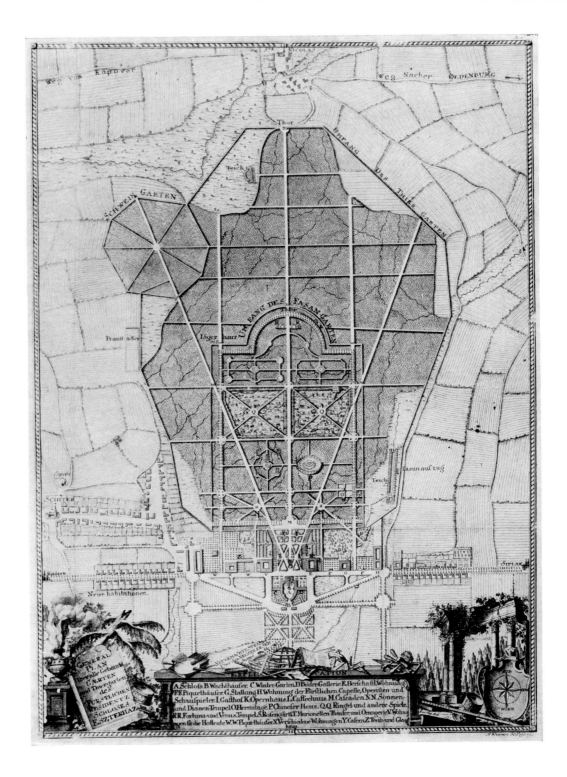

The control of the marshland of the Fertő Lake, which reached up to the castle, and
the construction of dams put a heavy burden on those in the Prince's service. Taxes
were trebled. Many peasants were compelled to sell their houses. Through rebuilding
and extending the hunting lodge at Süttör, built around 1720, Prince Nikolaus 'the
Magnificent' created perhaps the most beautiful and splendid castle in contemporary
Hungary. The main building was finished in 1766. From then on, Haydn's ensemble
spent the months from spring to autumn in the new residence which was already called
'Eszterháza'. However, only in 1784 did Prince Nikolaus consider the building of the
castle with its splendid park, fountains, pleasure houses, two theatres, guest-houses and
service flats, finished. A contemporary 'Description' and plan give an idea of the splen-
dour and of the cost of Eszterháza.

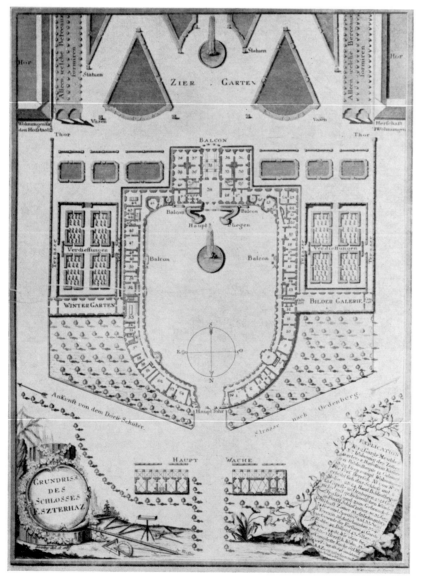

68 The side entrance
to the Palace, seen from
the 'music house'

69 Ground plan of
the Palace

A two-storey building on the road to
Széplak served to house the opera-
singers, musicians and actors. It may
be seen from a list dated 1782 that two
rooms with a kitchen were allotted
to the Kapellmeister, Haydn.

PROSPECT DER FÜRSTLICHEN RESIDENZ ESZTERHAZ VON DEN
HAUPT THOR GEGEN NORDEN.

J. Landerer Sc.

70–71 VIEW OF THE
COURTYARD OF THE
PALACE, AND THE FAÇADE
ONTO THE PARK

PROSPECT NACH DEM GARTEN UND WALD GEGEN SÜDEN.

45

**Beſchreibung**

des

Hochfürſtlichen

**Schloſſes Eſterhaß**

im

Königreiche Ungern.

Preßburg,
bey Anton Löwe, Buchdrucker und Buchhändler.
1784.

---

35

**Opernhaus.**

Gleich beym Eintritte in daſſelbe, führet eine ſehr anſehnliche Hauptſtiege, mit doppelten Aufgängen, und zierlichen eiſernen Geländern, zu zween Eingängen in die Fürſtliche Hauptloge, und zugleich auf die Gallerie. Nebenher ſind beyderſeits Kabineter, mit den daran befindlichen Retiraden. *Man ſehe die VII. Kupfertafel.*

Dieſe Hauptloge, wird durch roht marmorirte Römiſche Säulen, die bis auf den dritten Theil mit vergoldeten Stäben verziert, deren Schäfte, und Kapitäler aber ganz vergoldt ſind, unterſtüzet.

Der Platfond iſt ſehr niedlich gemalt, die Gallerie aber mit gepuzten Fußtafeln, und mit Römiſchen Wandpfeilern ausgeſchmückt, deren Stellung beyderſeits drey Kabineter formiren, zwiſchen welchen zween groſſe Trümeaur ſtehen. Die Tiſche unter denſelben ſind von Marmor, auf denſelben aber koſtbare Uhren, und Vaſen von Indianiſchem Porcellän, auch nebenher vergoldete prächtige Armleuchter.

E 2          Dieſe

---

## THE OPERA-HOUSE

*Straight from the entrance, an impressive double main staircase with graceful iron railings leads to the Prince's royal box and also to the gallery. The stairs are flanked by chambers on both sides.*

*This main box is supported by red marble Roman columns, decorated with golden rods up to a third of their height and completely gilded pillars and capitals. The ceiling is handsomely painted; the gallery is decorated with plastered flagstones, the positions of which form three chambers on both sides, which enclose two large trumeaux. The tables beneath these are made of marble, with precious clocks and vases of Indian porcelain standing on them, splendid gilt chandeliers alongside.*

*This gallery rests on pillars rising from the ground in a semi-circle. The balustrade is wholly gilt-lined with crimson leather, with other decorations also heavily gilded. At the front of the theatre there are also round boxes on both sides, behind which there are very prettily decorated chambers, equipped very expensively with fireplaces, couches, mirrors, clocks, and other necessities. These boxes, too, have separate entrances from outside.*

*The pit, with three adjoining entrances, holds an audience of four hundred.*

*The theatre is heated by four white stoves fitted at the sides. The colour scheme is mainly red marble, green and gold; the excellent lighting is provided by mirror sconces.*

*The external façade is decorated with Roman pillars and five round bow windows, three of which project. It has a balcony resting on plain Ionic columns, and this may be entered from the chambers at the back. It is ornamented with groups of genii beating kettledrums and blowing trumpets, and also with vases and festoons.*

*The theatre proper is of considerable width and depth. Behind it there are two dressing-rooms for the actors, with an exceedingly splendid and rich wardrobe.*

*Italian opera, seria and buffa, and German comedies are played on alternate days. The Prince is always present, and six o'clock is the usual time. The delight for eyes and ears is indescribable. It comes first from the music, since the entire orchestra resounds as a complete entity; now the most moving tenderness, now the most vehement power penetrates*

72–74 TITLE-PAGE, DESCRIPTION, AND PICTURE OF THE OPERA-HOUSE FROM THE 'DESCRIPTION OF THE PRINCE'S PALACE OF ESZTERHÁZA IN THE KINGDOM OF HUNGARY' DATED 1784

75 THE OPERA-HOUSE'S PLAN OF ITS CENTRAL HEATING

46

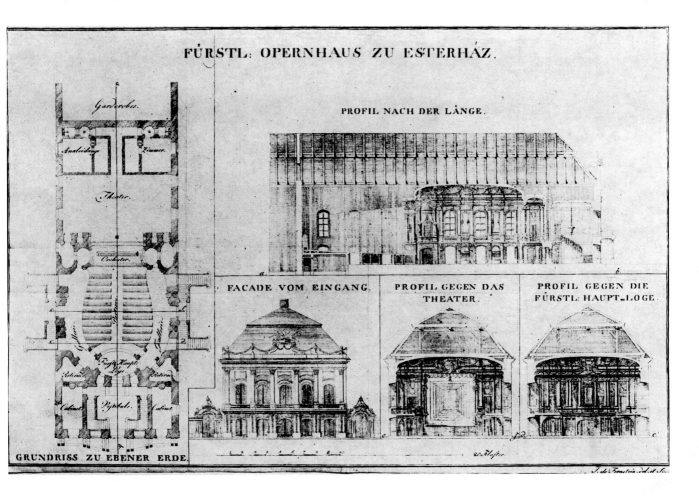

FÜRSTL: OPERNHAUS ZU ESTERHÁZ.

PROFIL NACH DER LÄNGE.

FACADE VOM EINGANG. PROFIL GEGEN DAS THEATER. PROFIL GEGEN DIE FÜRSTL: HAUPT-LOGE.

GRUNDRISS ZU EBENER ERDE.

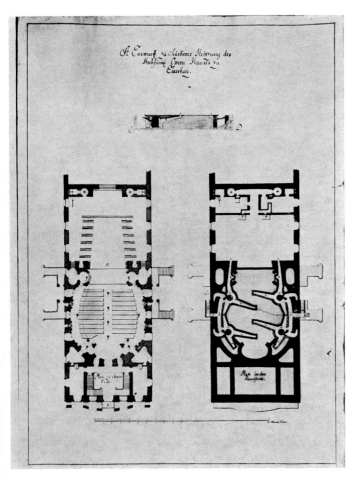

the soul—because the great musician, Herr Haiden, who serves the Prince as Kapellmeister, is the director. It comes also from the excellent lighting, the striking scenery, where clouds with deities slowly descend from above or ascend from below and disappear in a second, and then everything changes into a charming garden, magic forest or splendid hall.

Next to this opera house there is a well-equipped coffee-house.

## THE PUPPET THEATRE

This is opposite the opera and is quite spacious, but has no boxes or gallery. The entire pit resembles a grotto; all walls, niches and openings are covered with various materials, stones, shells, and snails, and when fully lit, these create a very unusual and striking effect.

The theatre is quite spacious, the decoration handsome, the puppets well made and splendidly dressed. Not only farces and comedies, but opera seria are also performed here; the late Maria Theresa graciously applauded the opera Alceste, and admired the sudden and unobservable transformations. The Siege of Gibraltar was also performed with great art and arrangement.—This is perhaps the only theatre of its kind in existence.

Anybody may enjoy the performances in this theatre as well as in the opera free of charge.

Close to the puppet theatre there are numerous splendid orangeries and other hothouses. (Description . . . 1784)

47

The opera building, which, though small, was fitted with all the most up-to-date technical devices, became known all over Europe within a few years. The art-loving nobility from near and far took their places in the boxes, while places in the pit were available to everyone, townspeople and peasants, without payment. It was described by the Hungarian occasional poet, Márton Dallos:

*This Place merits loitering a-while,*
*Who goes in? To guess, it's worth a try.*
*After beholding Play and Dance a-plenty,*
*We shall hear Music play'd quite excellently.*

*In their twos and threes, or even in their fours,*
*Some come with steady gait, others on a Horse,*
*Scholar, Noble, Peasant, each among his Friends,*
*Also Magyars, Germans, French and Italians.*

*One gropes for his Snuff blindly with his hand,*
*Sniffs while whisp'ring Scandal to his Friend,*
*Another flirts about freely with her fan,*
*Glancing behind it at one or other Man.*

*Here you can enter with no payment to meet,*
*And follow your Fancy in choosing any Seat,*
*And should it please you so, leave before it's ended,*
*For all do as they like in this Theatre splendid.*

48

The building of the opera-house brought new duties for Haydn—he had to compose operas. The series opened with two comic operas, for which the libretto had been supplied by Goldoni. The first performance of *Lo speziale* took place on the inauguration of the opera-house in 1768, *Le pescatrici* followed in September 1770, on the occasion of the wedding of the Countess Lamberg, one of the Prince's nieces. But such new duties meant also new opportunities: to venture into the genre of opera and to master theatrical music.

77 HOLOGRAPH OF THE LAST BARS OF THE OPERA 'LO SPEZIALE' (HOBOKEN XXVIII: 3)

78 HOLOGRAPH OF THE OPENING BARS OF LINDORO'S PASSIONATE ARIA IN D MINOR ('VARCA IL MARDI SPONDA IN SPONDA...') FROM THE OPERA 'LE PESCATRICI' (HOBOKEN XXVIII: 4)

THE FIRST PORTRAIT OF HAYDN

79 JOSEPH HAYDN IN
THE LIVERY OF THE
ESTERHÁZY MUSICIANS;
THE FIRST HAYDN
PORTRAIT, REPUTED TO
BE AUTHENTIC, BY
J. B. GRUNDMANN,
FROM AROUND 1768

50

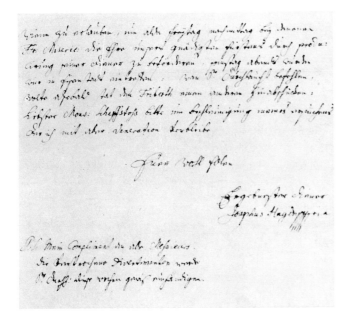

80 LAST PAGE OF HAYDN'S
LETTER ABOUT THE
'STABAT MATER' TO THE
PRINCE'S SECRETARY AND
PRINCIPAL BOOK-KEEPER,
ANTON SCHEFFSTOSS

81 JOHANN ADOLF HASSE
(1699–1783), THE FIRST
AMONG NOTABLE
CONTEMPORARY MUSICIANS
TO APPRECIATE HAYDN'S
ART AFTER HEARING HIS
'STABAT MATER' IN 1767

*Nobly born,*
*Highly respected Sir!*
*You will recall that last year I set to music with all my power the highly esteemed hymn,*
*called Stabat Mater, and that I sent it to the great and world-celebrated Hasse, with no other*
*intention than that in case, here and there, I had not expressed adequately words of such*
*great importance, this lack could be rectified by a master so successful in all forms of music.*
*But contrary to my merits, this unique artist honoured the work by inexpressible praise,*
*and wished nothing more than to hear it performed with the good players it requires. Since,*
*however, there is a great want of singers* utriusque generis *in Vienna, I would therefore*
*humbly and obediently ask His Serene and Gracious Highness through you, Sir, to allow*
*me, Weigl and his wife, and Friberth to go to Vienna next Thursday, stay there on Friday*
*afternoon at the FFr.: Miseric: to further the honour of our gracious prince by the per-*
*formance of his servant; we would return to Eisenstadt on Saturday evening.*
*If His Highness so wishes, someone other than Friberth could easily be sent up. Dearest*
*Mons. Scheffstoss, please expedite my request; I remain, with the most veneration,*

> *Your nobly born Sir's*
> *most devoted*
> *Josephus Haydn [m.]pria.*
> (Haydn, Eisenstadt, 20 March, 1768.)

82 ZWETTL (LOWER
AUSTRIA), WHERE
HAYDN'S 'APPLAUSUS'
CANTATA
(HOBOKEN XXIVA: 6)
WAS PERFORMED,
PROBABLY IN 1768

*First, I would ask you to observe strictly the tempi of all the arias and recitatives... Thirdly: in the accompanied recitatives, you must observe that the accompaniment should not enter until the singer has quite finished his text, even though the score often shows the contrary. For instance, at the beginning where the word 'metamorphosis' is repeated and the orchestra comes in at '-phosis', you must nevertheless wait until the last syllable is finished and then enter quickly; for it would be ridiculous if you would fiddle away the word from the singer's mouth, and understand only the words 'quae metamo-'. But I leave this to the harpsichord player, and all the others must follow him... Fourthly: that the fortes and pianos are written correctly throughout, and should be observed exactly; for there is a very great difference between* piano *and* pianissimo, forte *and* fortiss[imo], *between* crescendo *and* forzando *and so forth... Fifthly: I have often been annoyed at certain violinists in various concerts, who absolutely ruined the so-called ties—which are among the most beautiful things in music—in that they bounced the bows off the tied note, which should have been joined to the preceding note. And so I would point [this] out to the first violinist... Sixthly: I would ask you to use two players on the viola part throughout, for the inner parts sometimes need to be heard more than the upper parts, and you will find in all my compositions that the viola rarely doubles the bass... Ninthly: I hope for at least three or four rehearsals for the entire work. Tenthly: in the soprano aria the bassoon can be omitted if absolutely necessary, but I would rather have it present, at least when the bass is* obbligato *throughout. And I prefer a band with 3 bass instruments—'cello, bassoon and double-bass—to one with 6 double-basses and 3 'celli, because certain passages stand out better that way...*

(From Haydn's letter concerning
the performance of his
*Applausus* Cantata, 1768)

52

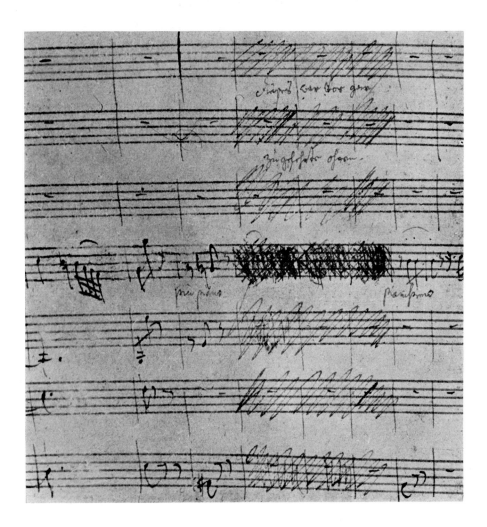

83 FROM THE MANUSCRIPT
OF THE SLOW MOVEMENT
OF THE SYMPHONY IN
D MAJOR
(HOBOKEN I: 42)
FROM 1771

*Dieses war vor gar zu gelehrte ohren* [This was for over-educated ears]. Haydn was amused by those who criticized his bold artistic experiments.

But if he found a passage which demanded a far too 'educated' ear, his own judgment prompted his changes.

'*Have you ever made a system or rules,' I asked, 'with the help of which you could extort the certain approval of the public?' Haydn was silent, so I went on: 'You know,' I said, 'that our philosophers analyze everything and are not long satisfied for with "this pleases" until they have found the reason why this pleases? Once they have discovered the reason, they then know the component parts of the beautiful and can govern the latter by rules, which anyone who means to produce something that will please must observe as strictly as possible.' Haydn answered: 'In the heat of composition I never thought about that. I wrote what seemed to me good, and corrected it afterwards according to the rules of harmony. Other devices I have never made use of. Several times I took the liberty, not of offending the ear of course, but of breaking the usual textbook rules, and wrote beneath these places the words* con licenza. *Some cried out: "A mistake!" and tried to prove it by citing Fux. I asked my critics whether they could prove by ear that it was a mistake? They had to answer No.'* (Dies)

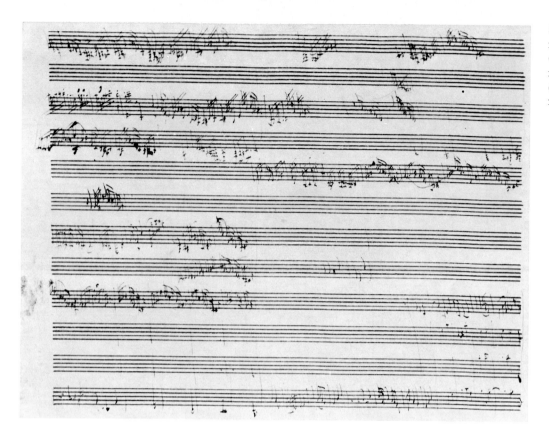

From the quantity of his compositions, one might conclude that Haydn must have worked very easily. This was not the case. 'I was never a fast writer, and always composed with deliberation and industry. Such works, however, are made to last, and this is at once revealed to the connoisseur by the score. When Cherubini looked through several of my manuscripts, he always hit on the places that deserve respect' ... Haydn always worked out his compositions as a whole. He laid out the entire plan of the principal voice in each part, marking the main places by small notes or numbers; afterwards he breathed spirit and life into the dry skeleton through the other accompanying voices and dexterous transitions. His scores are clean and clearly written, and corrections are seldom found in them. 'This is because I do not write until I am sure of the thing.' (Griesinger)

86 Manuscript of the
last bars of the slow
movement from the
String Quartet in
G minor, Opus 20
(Hoboken III: 33)

After the rural seclusion of the residence at Eszterháza, the few winter weeks spent in Vienna became very important for Haydn's artistic development. He was on friendly terms with Florian Leopold Gassmann, who catalogued the Imperial Hofbibliothek at the beginning of the 1770s. This collection was a treasure-trove of great baroque music, and held, among other things, numerous scores by Handel. Perhaps these external influences also contributed to the final maturing of experiments that Haydn carried out over half a decade, towards a wholly personal style in which polyphonic and homophonic composition, and the major and minor keys had become of equal importance for the first time since the death of J. S. Bach and Handel. (The six String Quartets of Opus 20, the *Funeral* Symphony No. 44, the *Farewell* Symphony No. 45, the C-minor Symphony No. 52, the C-minor Sonata for piano, Hoboken XVI: 20 etc.)

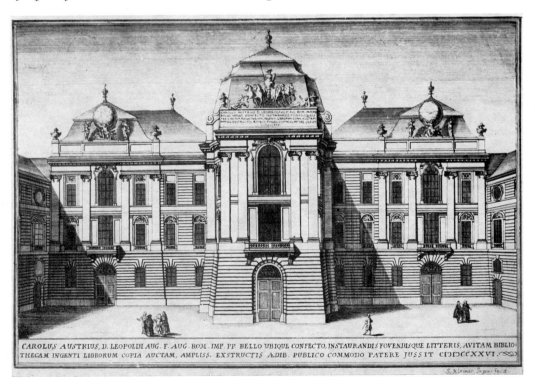

CAROLUS AUSTRIUS, D. LEOPOLDI AUG. F. AUG. ROM. IMP. PP. BELLO UBIQUE CONFECTO, INSTAURANDIS FOVENDISQUE LITTERIS, AVITAM BIBLIO-THECAM INGENTI LIBRORUM COPIA AUCTAM, AMPLISS. EXSTRUCTIS ADIB. PUBLICO COMMODO PATERE JUSSIT CIƆIƆCCXXVI.

88–91 The last four pages of the manuscript of the 'Farewell' Symphony in F sharp minor (Hoboken I: 45) 1772

In Prince Esterházy's orchestra were several vigorous young married men who in summer, when the Prince stayed at Esterháza castle, had to leave their wives behind in Eisenstadt. Contrary to his custom, the Prince once wished to extend his stay in Esterháza by several weeks. The fond husbands, particularly dismayed at this news, turned to Haydn and pleaded with him to do something. Haydn had the notion of writing a symphony (known as the Farewell Symphony) in which one instrument after the other is silent. This symphony was performed at the first opportunity in the presence of the Prince, and each of the musicians was directed, as soon as his part was finished, to put out his candle, pack up his music and, with his instrument under his arm, to go away. The Prince and the audience understood the meaning of this pantomime at once, and the next day came the order to depart from Esterháza. Thus Haydn told me the origin of the Farewell Symphony; and the variant, that Haydn thereby dissuaded his Prince from the intention of disbanding his whole orchestra and thus reassured many men of their livelihood, is to be sure, poetically more attractive, but not historically correct. (Griesinger)

'I was then young and gay and consequently no better than the rest,' said Haydn with a smile. Prince Nikolaus must long since have guessed the secret wishes of his musicians. Their comic goings on have even amused him. Otherwise how could he have taken it into his head this time to lengthen by two months the usual six months' residence? . . . An ordinary man in such cases plays a silly prank, a man of talent finds a way out. Haydn had recourse to his muse, and sketched a sextet of a new sort. On an evening soon after, Prince Nikolaus was surprised in the most wonderful way with this music. Right in the middle of the most passionate music, one voice ends; the player silently closes his part, takes his instrument, puts out the lights, and goes off. Soon after, a second voice ends; the player behaves the same

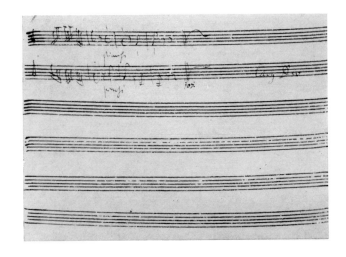

as the first, and withdraws. Now a third ends; a fourth voice; all put out their lights and take their instruments away with them. The orchestra grows dark and increasingly deserted. The Prince and all the audience maintain a wondering silence. Finally the last man but one, Haydn himself, puts out his lights, takes his music, and withdraws. A single violinist is left. Haydn had picked him to be last on purpose, because his solo playing pleased the Prince greatly, and he would be almost forced by the art of this player to wait for the end. The end came, the last lights were put out and Tomasini also went off.—The Prince now stood up and said: 'If they all go off, we must go too.' The musicians had meanwhile collected in the ante-chamber, where the Prince found them and smiling said: 'I understand', Haydn; tomorrow the men may all leave', whereupon he gave the necessary orders to have the princely horses and carriages prepared for the journey. The truth of the tales of the ancients concerning the wondrous workings of music upon the emotions has often been doubted, but I do not understand the basis of this doubt. The instrumental music of the ancients always served as accompaniment to singing or to mimic dancing. One would have to cast doubts, as well, therefore, on the powerful workings of song and of dance and so on, which, after all, experience still bears out every day. Had Haydn undertaken without singing, without dancing, without acting, solely through the power of melody and harmony, to work on the Prince's feelings, to make himself understood, and to accomplish his purpose, it seems to me he would have undertaken an impossibility. Granted that instrumental music stirs the emotions. What language then can boast of having found words for those emotions? Music without the addition of words, of dancing or of acting is a riddle to the intellect, capable of an infinity of meanings. Thus Haydn wisely had recourse to acting. The putting out of the lights, the going away, and the like, were actions that spoke to assist the music and earn it the nickname Farewell Symphony. (Dies)

*Most Serene and Noble Prince of the Holy Roman Empire,*
*Gracious and dread Lord!*
*Your Highness intimated to me, through His Highness' secretary Schefstoss, that you would*
*be minded graciously and generously to provide a year's salary to me and to those chamber*
*musicians who entered the service of Your Serene Highness' brother (provided that each of*
*us would submit a petition to that effect to Your Highness).*
*May I therefore ask, in profound submissiveness, that Your Highness confirm, in your*
*infinite kindness, your willingness to grant us this exceptionally gracious mark of esteem.*
*For this, I shall offer you at all times my most faithful services, and I recommend myself*
*to your serene favour and grace.*

> *Your Serene Highness'*
> *most humble*
> *Joseph Haydn*
> Capell-Meister

*If there is no counter-claim, the suppliant should be paid one year's salary according to the*
*contract then in force, minus 10 percent inheritance tax; this sum is to be paid out by our*
*Chief Cashier's Office, but the sum for the inheritance tax is to be delivered to Doctor Son-*
*leithner after securing the necessary receipt.*
*Vienna, 1st April 1773.*

> *Nicolaus Fürst Esterházy*

(Haydn's application with a note by the Prince)

93 Pay-sheet of the
musicians
in February, 1772.
The name of the
Kapellmeister, Joseph
Haydn, heads the list

94 Haydn's receipt.
Only eleven years
after the death of his
predecessor did
Prince Nikolaus pay
the amount bequeathed
to the musicians

95 HUNGARIAN GYPSIES PLAYING MUSIC IN THE COURTYARD OF THE PALACE AT ESZTERHÁZA

96 'GYPSY DANCES' IN A HUNGARIAN DANCE COLLECTION (FOR VIOLIN) DATING FROM THE 18TH CENTURY

97 THE VIOLIN PART OF THE 'MENUETTO ALLA ZINGARESE' FROM THE HAYDN QUARTET IN D MAJOR, OPUS 20, No. 4 (HOBOKEN III: 34), 1772

The influence of contemporary Hungarian music is noticeable in Haydn's instrumental colouring in several melodic themes. He was influenced mainly by popular melodies played by gypsy musicians, and also by genuine Hungarian folk songs and folk dances which were presented by the peasants on the estates as curiosities for the foreign guests.

98 DETAIL OF 95.
THE GYPSY BAND
CONSISTED OF VIOLIN,
VIOLA, VIOLONCELLO
AND CIMBALOM

Hungarian traits can be found in Haydn's music right up to his final compositions. In the last years of his life he virtually lost direct contact with Hungarian music, but the stimulus of the earlier years lived on in his memory. Perhaps he also came across the scores of some Hungarian music. The Viennese publishers Traeg even put out, in 1799, a series of *Zingarese* under Joseph Haydn's name.

99 ONE OF THE LAST
'HUNGARISMS'
THE FINALE
'RONDO AL'ONGARESA'
FROM THE G-MAJOR TRIO
(HOBOKEN XV: 25),
AROUND 1795

100 THE LAST HAYDN
COMPOSITION, WHICH ONLY
REFERRED TO HUNGARY
IN ITS TITLE, THE
'HUNGARIAN
NATIONAL MARCH'
(HOBOKEN VIII: 4), 1802

From 1768 theatrical groups were employed permanently to perform at Eszterháza. The theatre companies of Hellmann and Koberwein, Passer, and above all the group of Carl Wahr, created an outstanding theatrical life in the Prince's residence (1772–1777). Shakespeare's *Hamlet*, *Macbeth*, *Othello*, *King Lear*, Lessing's *Emilia Galotti*, *Minna von Barnhelm*, Goethe's *Clavigo*, *Stella*, the guest performance of the famous French ballet dancer, Noverre, all brought distant cultures to Haydn in his exile.

CARL WAHR

101 (LEFT) MARCO COLTELLINI (AROUND 1740–1775), WHO IS SUPPOSED TO HAVE WRITTEN THE LIBRETTO FOR HAYDN'S OPERA 'L'INFEDELTÀ DELUSA' (HOBOKEN XXVIII: 5), 1773

102 (ABOVE RIGHT) THE BALLET DANCER JEAN GEORGES NOVERRE (1727–1810)

103 THE THEATRE MANAGER CARL WAHR

104 GOUACHE PAINTING
OF AN OPERATIC
PERFORMANCE SUPPOSED
TO REPRESENT A
PRODUCTION AT
ESZTERHÁZA

In this famous painting the director (Haydn?) sits at the cembalo and conducts his orchestra. The painting offers a glimpse of the artistic and technical equipment of small theatres of the period, which even made it possible for an actor to appear in the clouds if necessary, with the help of lifting devices. The elaborate scenery illustrates the preference for oriental-exotic subjects. One can see the seating arrangement of the musicians in the orchestra, and the director leading his orchestra from the cembalo.

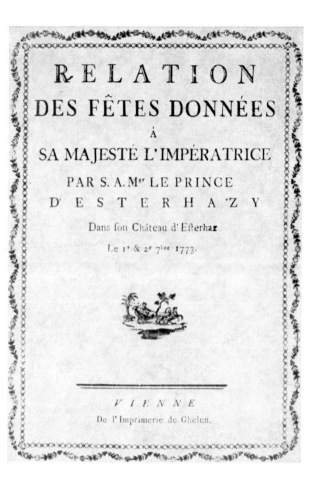

'If I want to hear a good opera, I go to Eszterháza.' These frequently quoted words of Maria Theresa's were based on the experience of one visit to Eszterháza. The high point of the first day (1st September, 1773) was the revival of the opera *L'infedeltà delusa*; of the second day, the dancing of several thousand Hungarian peasants to their own music.

105 (RIGHT) COMMEMORATIVE DESCRIPTION OF THE VISIT OF MARIA THERESA TO ESZTERHÁZA (1773)

106 (LEFT) THE CHINESE PLEASURE-HOUSE (BAGATELLE) CONSTRUCTED FOR THE EMPRESS' VISIT, WHERE HAYDN DIRECTED BEFORE MARIA THERESA HIS SYMPHONY ('MARIA THERESA', HOBOKEN I: 48)

107 EMPRESS MARIA THERESA IN 1770

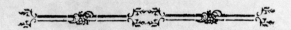

# Philemon und Baucis.

## Oder

### Jupiters Reise

#### auf die Erde.

Bey Gelegenheit
der höchsterfreulichen Gegenwart
Allerhöchst

## Jhro k. k. apostol. Majestät

und
Allerhöchst dero allerdurchlauchtigsten

### Erzhauses.

In einer Marionetten Operette zum erstenmale

#### zu Esterház

auf der fürstlichen Marionetten Bühne
im Jahre 1773. aufgeführt.

FERDINAND
Königl. Prinz von Ungarn und Böhmen
Erzherzog von Oesterreich,
Fürst von Salzburg, Eichstädt, Berchtolsgaden
und Passau.

108 LIBRETTO OF
HAYDN'S PUPPET-OPERA
'PHILEMON AND BAUCIS'
(HOBOKEN XXIX: 1)

109 ARCHDUKE
FERDINAND (1754–1806)

In August 1775 Haydn's company once again became the centre of attention: the composer conducted his new opera *L'incontro improvviso* before a number of select guests, headed by the Habsburg Archduke Ferdinand and Beatrice d'Este. The puppet theatre was also one of the most charming attractions of Eszterháza. During Maria Theresa's sojourn, on the second day of her visit, Haydn's puppet-opera *Philemon and Baucis* was performed, with splendid scenery. Haydn himself owned a number of puppets which were borrowed by the Prince in the spring of 1775, when he wished to present a birthday surprise to his wife.

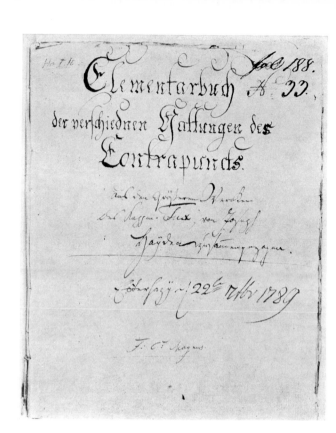

## HAYDN'S DISCIPLES

Haydn's steadily increasing reputation and the successes of his works brought him his first pupils in composition. Haydn's circle of disciples consisted mainly of the Prince's musicians (P. Niemecz, J. G. Distler, J. B. Krumpholtz, A. Kraft, F. A. Rosetti). The talented Ignaz Pleyel was sent to him with a scholarship from the Hungarian Count Ladislaus Erdődy. (As a token of his satisfaction with Haydn's teaching, the Count presented the master with a carriage and pair.)

110 IGNAZ PLEYEL
(1757–1831)

111–112 TITLE-PAGE
AND PART OF A
COUNTERPOINT TEXTBOOK
DICTATED BY HAYDN
TO HIS DISCIPLE
F. C. MAGNUS,
MAKING USE OF THE
'GRADUS AD PARNASSUM'
BY J. J. FUX

Vüe du Theatre dela Courprés dela porté de Carinthie . N.º 28. auf dem Graben N.º 7200 bey Maria Geissler. Ansicht des k.k. Theater nächst dem Kärntner Th

## SUCCESS OF THE TOBIAS ORATORIO IN VIENNA (1775)

*Il ritorno di Tobia* (Hoboken XXI: 1), the first large-scale oratorio by Joseph Haydn, was performed on the 2nd and 4th April 1775, at the concert of the Vienna 'Tonkünstler-Sozietät'. The performance took place at the Kärntnertor Theatre with Haydn himself directing. He had brought with him the Friberths, both singers, the viol-player and bass Specht, the violinist Tomasini, and Marteau the violoncellist from Eszterháza. (Haydn, though he did not live in Vienna, applied later for admission to the 'Tonkünstler-Sozietät'. However, the jealous wrangling of his colleagues hampered his admission so long that he withdrew his application. Indeed, the Society admitted Haydn as a member only in 1797.)

*The famous Kapellmeister, Herr Hayden, has had great success with the performance of the oratorio entitled* The return of Tobias *on the second and fourth of the current month, and he has again displayed his well-known skill to its best advantage. Expression, nature and art were spun so finely throughout his work that his listeners had to love the one and admire the other. His choirs especially glowed with a fire which had previously belonged only to Handel; in short, the entire unusually large audience was delighted, and Hayden became the great artist whose works were loved by the whole of Europe, and whose original genius was recognized far and wide.* (K. k. priv. Realzeitung der Wissenschaften, 1775/14)

114 THE FIRST PAGE OF
THE MANUSCRIPT OF THE
AUTOBIOGRAPHICAL
SKETCH. IN 1776 HAYDN
WAS ASKED TO WRITE
HIS CURRICULUM VITAE
FOR 'DAS GELEHRTE
ÖSTERREICH'

*Estoras, 6th July 1776.*

*Mademoiselle!*
*You will not take it amiss, if I hand you a hotchpotch of all sorts of things as an answer to your request: to describe such things properly takes time, and that I don't have; for this reason, I do not dare write to Mons. Zoller personally, and therefore ask forgiveness.*
*I send you only a rough draft, for neither pride, nor fame, but solely the great kindness and marked satisfaction that so learned a national institution has shown towards my previous compositions, have induced me to comply with their demand.*
*I was born on the last day of March 1733, in the market town of Rohrau, Lower Austria, near Prugg on the Leythä. My late father was a wheelwright by profession, and served Count Harrach, great lover of music by nature. He [my father] played the harp without knowing a note of music, and as a boy of five, I correctly sang all his simple little pieces; this induced my father to entrust me to the care of my relative, the schoolmaster in Haimburg, in order that I might learn the rudiments of music and the other juvenile acquirements. Almighty God (to Whom alone I owe the most profound gratitude) endowed me, especially in music, with such proficiency that even in my 6th year I was able to sing some masses in the choir-loft and to play a little on the harpsichord and violin.*

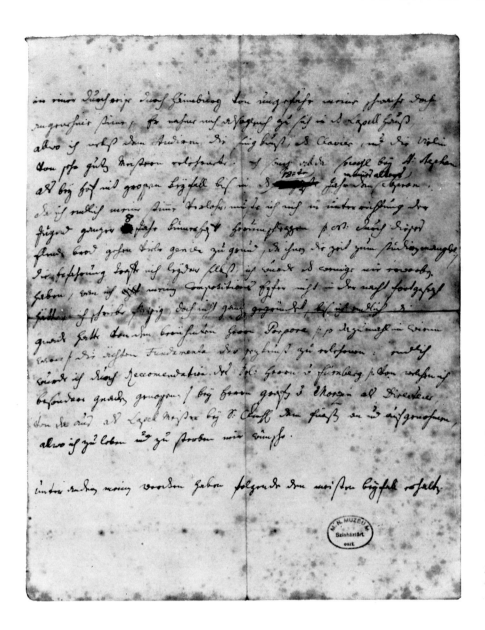

When I was 7, the late Capellmeister *von Reutter* passed through Haimburg and quite accidentally heard my weak but pleasant voice. He forthwith took me away to the choir house [of St. Stephen's Cathedral in Vienna] where, apart from my studies, I learnt the art of singing, the harpsichord, and the violin, from very good masters. Until my 18th year I sang soprano with great success, not only at St. Stephen's but also at the Court. Finally I lost my voice, and then had to eke out a wretched existence for eight whole years, by teaching young pupils (many geniuses are ruined by their having to earn their daily bread, because they have no time to study): I experienced this, too, and would have never learnt what little I did, had I not, in my zeal for composition, composed well into the night; I wrote diligently, but not quite correctly, until at last I had the good fortune to learn the true fundamentals of composition from the celebrated Herr Porpora (who was at that time in Vienna): finally, by the recommendation of the late Herr von Fürnberg (from whom I received many marks of favour), I was engaged as Directeur at Herr von Morzin's, and from there as Capellmeister of His Highness the Prince [Esterházy], in whose service I wish to live and die. Inter alia *the following compositions of mine have received the most approbation:*

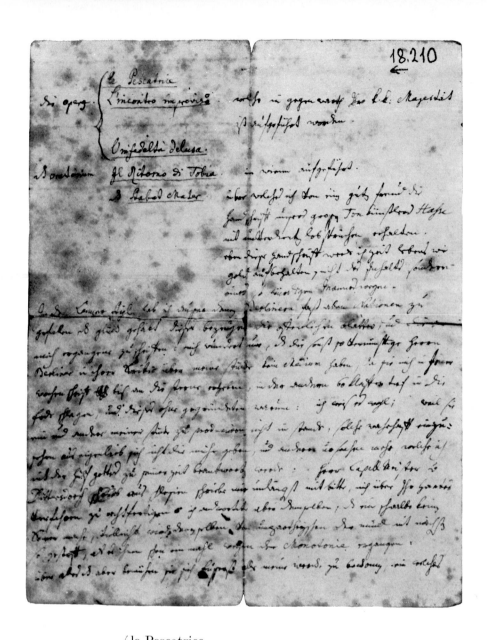

| The operas | le Pescatrice | |
| | L'incontro improviso | *performed in the presence of Her Imperial and Royal Majesty.* |
| | l'infedeltà delusa | |
| The oratorio | Il Ritorno di Tobia | *performed in Vienna.* |
| | The Stabat Mater, | *about which I received (through a good friend) a testimonial of our great composer Hasse, containing quite undeserved eulogiums. I shall treasure this testimonial all my life, as if it were gold; not for its contents, but for the sake of so admirable a man.* |

*In the chamber-musical style I have been fortunate enough to please almost all nations except the Berliners; this is shown by the public newspapers and letters addressed to me. I only wonder that the Berlin gentlemen, who are otherwise so reasonable, preserve no medium in their criticism of my music, for in one weekly paper they praise me to the skies, while in another they dash me sixty fathoms deep into the earth, and this without explaining why; though I know very well why: because they are incapable of performing some of my works, and are too conceited to take the trouble to understand them properly, and for other reasons which, with God's help, I will answer in good time. Herr Capellmeister von Dittersdorf, in Silesia, wrote to me recently and asked me to defend myself against their hard words, but I answered that one swallow does not make the Summer; and that perhaps one of these days some unprejudiced person would stop their tongues, as happened to them once before, when they accused me of monotony. Despite this, they try very hard to get all my works, as Herr*

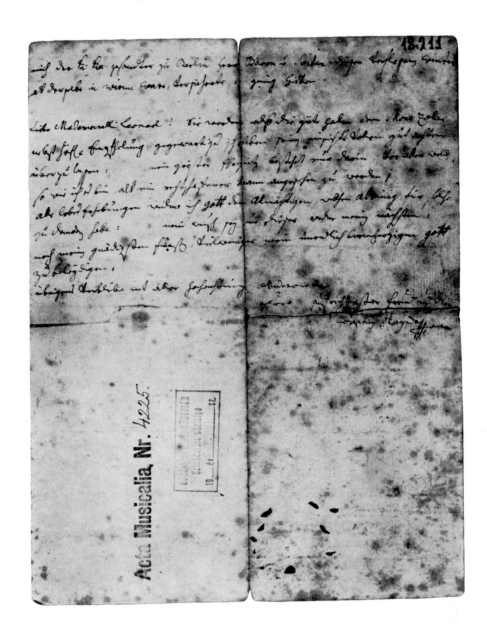

Baron von Sviten, the Imperial and Royal Ambassador at Berlin, told me only last winter,
when he was in Vienna: but enough of this.

Dear Mademoiselle Leonore: You will be good enough to give this present letter, and my
compliments, to Mons. Zoller for his consideration: my highest ambition is only that all the
world regard me as the honest man I am.

I offer all my praises to Almighty God, for I owe them to Him alone: my sole wish is to offend
neither my neighbour, nor my gracious Prince, nor above all our merciful God.

Meanwhile I remain, Mademoiselle, with high esteem,

Your most sincere friend and servant

Josephus Haydn [m.p.]ria

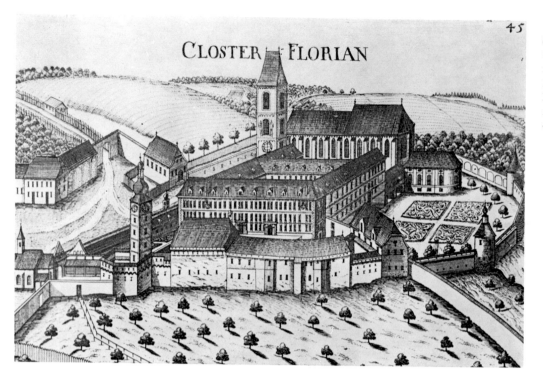

CLOSTER • FLORIAN

118 The monastery of St. Florian. Its library, like the libraries at Göttweig, Kremsmünster, Lambach and Melk, preserves many copies of Haydn's works

*He did not know himself how celebrated he was abroad, and he heard of it only occasionally from travelling foreigners who visited him. Many of these, even Gluck, advised him to travel to Italy and France, but his timidity and his limited circumstances held him back; if he spoke a word about it in the hearing of his Prince, the latter pressed a dozen ducats into his hand, and so he abandoned all such projects again. Haydn himself believed that because of his good foundation in singing and in instrumental accompaniment, he would have become an excellent opera composer, if he had had the fortune to go to Italy. The accident twice befell him of having his house in Eisenstadt burn down, and each time the Prince had it rebuilt. Several of Haydn's operas and other compositions were thus a prey of the flames, and there exists hardly a copy of them.* (Griesinger)

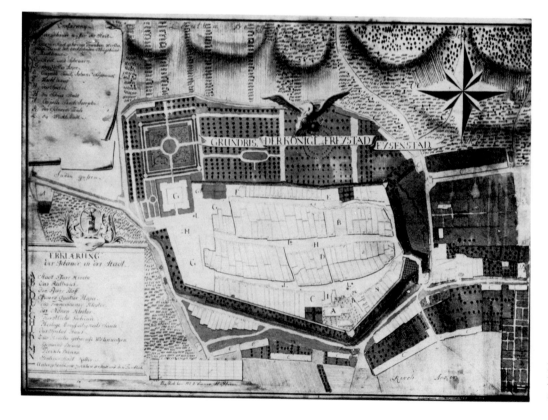

119 A map of Eisenstadt in 1778. Haydn lived in the street between E and F

120 THE MONASTERY
OF LAMBACH
121 THE MONASTERY
OF MELK

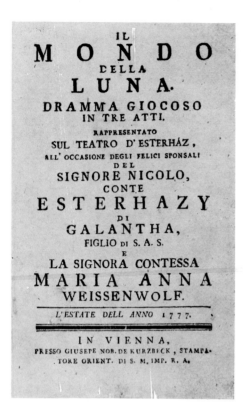

IL
# MONDO
DELLA
# LUNA.
DRAMMA GIOCOSO
IN TRE ATTI.
RAPPRESENTATO
SUL TEATRO D'ESTERHÁZ,
ALL' OCCASIONE DEGLI FELICI SPONSALI
DEL
SIGNORE NICOLO,
CONTE
# ESTERHAZY
DI
GALANTHA,
FIGLIO DI S. A. S.
E
LA SIGNORA CONTESSA
# MARIA ANNA
WEISSENWOLF.
L'ESTATE DELL ANNO 1777.

IN VIENNA,
PRESSO GIUSEPE NOB. DE KURZBECK, STAMPA-
TORE ORIENT. DI S. M. IMP. R. A.

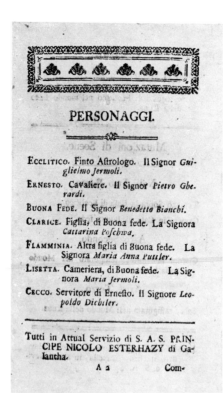

## PERSONAGGI.

ECCLITICO. Finto Aftrologo. Il Signor *Gui-glieimo Jermoli.*

ERNESTO. Cavaliere. Il Signor *Pietro Ghe-rardi.*

BUONA FEDE. Il Signor *Benedetto Bianchi.*

CLARICE. Figlia, di Buona fede. La Signora *Cattarina Pofchwa.*

FLAMMINIA. Altra figlia di Buona fede. La Signora *Maria Anna Puttler.*

LISETTA. Cameriera, di Buona fede. La Signora *Maria Jermoli.*

CECCO. Servitore di Ernefto. Il Signore *Leopoldo Dichtler.*

Tutti in Attual Servizio di S. A. S. PRIN-CIPE NICOLO ESTERHAZY di Ga-lantha.

A 2                    Com-

122–123 TITLE-PAGE AND
CAST-LIST FROM THE
LIBRETTO OF HAYDN'S
COMIC OPERA 'IL MONDO
DELLA LUNA'
(HOBOKEN XXVIII: 7),
WHICH HAD ITS FIRST
PERFORMANCE IN
ESZTERHÁZA IN
AUGUST 1777

124 CARLO GOLDONI
(1707–1793), WHO WROTE
THE LIBRETTO OF
THE OPERA
'LA VERA COSTANZA'
(HOBOKEN XXVIII: 8)

After the success of the *Tobias* Oratorio, the Vienna Court Opera asked Haydn to set to music the libretto of *La vera costanza*. The first performance planned for 1777 did not take place, because the better known and more popular Italian composer Pasquale Anfossi had completed his music for the same libretto before Haydn. Haydn's stage works cannot compete with the inventive dramaturgy and effusive musical richness of his Italian contemporaries, and in their musical character, they are also surpassed by Mozart's mature operas. They compensate, however, by their fine instrumentation, practically unknown in other stage music, their careful musical construction and also a symphonic style which reaches the highest form of instrumental music.

125 (LEFT) VINCENZO RIGHINI (1756–1812)

126 (RIGHT) PASQUALE ANFOSSI (1727–1797)

From the mid-seventies the Prince's interest in his favourite instrument, the baryton, noticeably lessened. But his interest in opera increased, and these could offer greater entertainment to distinguished guests at his splendid residence, the fame of which had spread far beyond the frontiers of his country. In 1776, he had operas performed twice weekly, and by the mid-1780s more than a hundred in any one theatrical season.

127 THE CAST-LIST AND FIRST PAGE OF THE LIBRETTO OF ANFOSSI'S OPERA 'LA FINTA GIARDINIERA' PERFORMED AT ESZTERHÁZA IN 1780

128 (LEFT) JOHANN
GOTTLIEB NAUMANN
(1741–1801)

129 (RIGHT)
ANTONIO SALIERI
(1750–1825)

The Prince's musical ensemble was strengthened by the appointment of famous Italian singers. This increasing 'operatic management' brought additional tasks and placed increasingly pressing burdens on Haydn. He had to do everything himself, from selecting the pieces to be performed to rehearsing the cast, and conducting every performance; sometimes he even had to copy out the parts by hand. All this was at the expense of his free time, which he should have spent in composition.

Haydn's pleasure in his work suffered from the preference of the Prince's guests for comic operas by contemporary Italian composers. It hurt him deeply that stereotyped, less carefully worked out music should be preferred to his own works. In fifteen years Haydn had to perform more than eighty operas by Anfossi, Bianchi, Cimarosa, Paisiello, Piccini, Sacchini, Salieri, Sarti, Righini, Traëtta, Zingarelli and others. It is not surprising that with unconcealed displeasure he shortened, re-wrote and re-instrumented the works of his rivals and that he inserted his own arias.

130 OPERATIC MATERIALS
CONDUCTED BY HAYDN,
IN THE ORIGINAL FOLIOS
OF THE FORMER
ESTERHÁZY COLLECTION

131 Court life at
Eszterháza
132 Libretto of a
Dittersdorf
performance
133 Libretto of
Haydn's opera
'La fedeltà premiata'
(Hoboken XXVIII: 10)

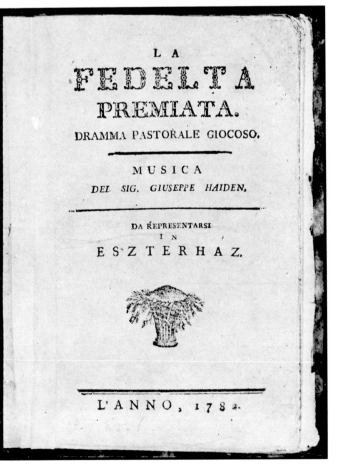

Montuosa ripiena di Nevi per l'opera l'Orlando

Pietro Travaglia, a gifted artist who
had studied in Milan and had considerable theatrical experience, was in
the service of Prince Esterházy from
the year 1771. His sketches of scenery provide a very vivid picture of
the stage of the Eszterháza opera-
house. The snowy landscape above
was designed by Travaglia for the
first performance of the opera *Orlando Paladino* in 1782, with a libretto by Nunziato Porta. In that
period, Haydn composed hardly any
operas; *Orlando* is in many respects a
pioneer work: an experiment leading
towards the 'dramma eroicomico'
and to the 'semiseria', that led to
Mozart's *Don Giovanni*.

## MUTAZZIONI DI SCENE.

### NELL' ATTO PRIMO.

Luogo magnifico deftinato per le publiche
udienze con trono da un lato. Veduta
in profpetto della Citta di Cartagine, che
sta in atto edificandofi.

Cortile.

Tempio di Nettuno con fimulacro del me-
defimo.

### NELL' ATTO SECONDO.

Appartamenti Reali con tauolino.

Atrio.

Gabinetto con fedie.

### NELL' ATTO TERZO.

Bofco preffo la Città.

Reggia con veduta della Città di Cartagine
in profpetto, che poi s'incendia.

___

*Le Decorazzioni fono del Sigr. Pietro Travaglia
Pittore Teatrale di S. A.*

A 3        PER-

135 Description of
Travaglia's stage
sets for Sarti's
'La Didone
abbandonata'

136–137 Two costume
designs for Haydn's
last opera composed
at Eszterháza, the
'Armida', which was
first performed in 1784
(Hoboken XXVIII: 12)

138 A stage set by
Travaglia

79

The paper Haydn used for writing his music for a long time came from the Prince's paper-mill in Lockenhaus. The usual watermark of the paper-mill, under the masters J. G. Schobenwalter, J. G. Wallner and O. Wenko was a stag; but occasionally, paper was produced also with the Esterházy coat of arms.

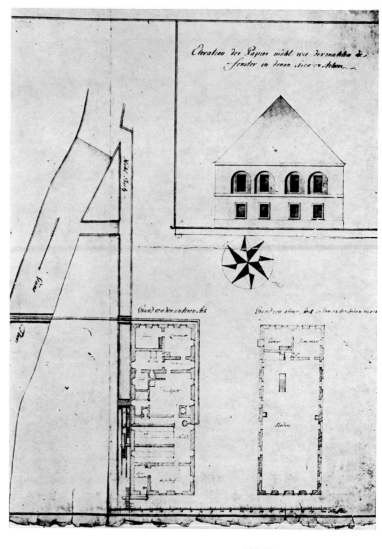

139 THE PAPER-MILL AT LOCKENHAUS

140–145 SOME WATERMARKS IN PAPER USED BY HAYDN

146 ‘Copied in twelve hours’—a note at the end of a first violin part by Johann Schellinger, chief copyist at the Prince's theatre

147 An invoice by Schellinger, approved by Haydn and by the Prince

# HAYDN'S COPYISTS IN ESZTERHÁZA

148 Joseph Elssler, sr. (d. 1782), Haydn's private copyist

149 Johann Schellinger (Schillinger), head of the copyists at the theatre

150 Joseph Elssler, jr. (?), who later became an oboist in the prince's orchestra

151 The writing of an unknown copyist, known from the extant copies of many works by Haydn

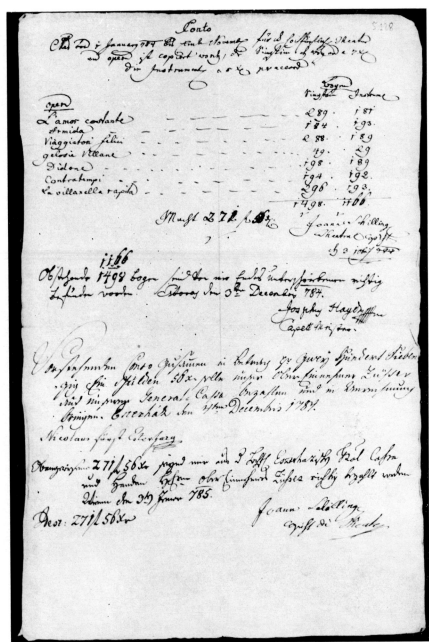

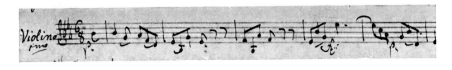

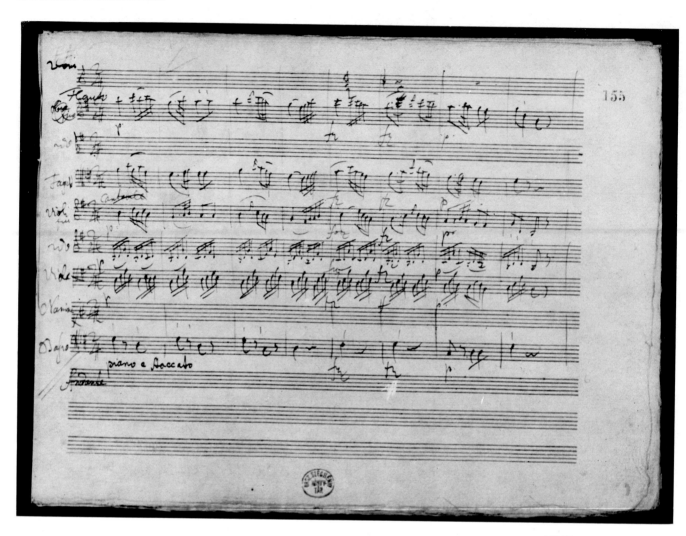

155

152 THE OPENING BARS
OF AN INSERTED ARIA
WRITTEN FOR LUIGIA
POLZELLI
153 COMPOSER AND
SINGER; A CONTEMPORARY
ENGRAVING

The nineteen-year-old Italian singer, Luigia
Polzelli (Polcelli, 1760–1832) and her elderly and
sickly husband, a violinist, were appointed to
Eszterháza in 1779. After one year, their contract was extended only on Haydn's intercession.
No picture has survived of Luigia, with whom
Haydn had a close relationship for years. According to the description in her passport, she had
a narrow, longish face and a dark complexion
with lively dark eyes; her eyebrows and hair
were chestnut, and she was of medium height
with an elegant figure. She was not particularly
gifted and her voice was not outstanding, merely
a modest mezzo-soprano. With moving tenderness, Haydn adapted parts to her capabilities.
The overwhelming majority of his inserted arias
between 1779 and 1790 were composed for her.

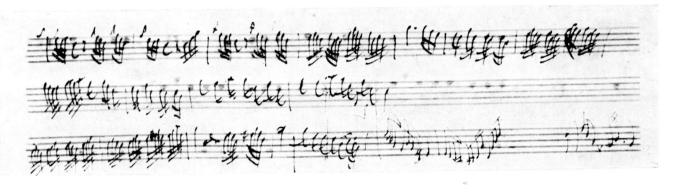

154 Coloratura sketch
for Luigia Polzelli

155 Haydn at forty-nine.
Engraving by Johann
Ernst Mansfeld (1781)

Many people are delighted with my portrait. Return the oil-portrait to me in the same case. (Haydn to Artaria, 27 May, 1781)
You once again make me your debtor for the portraits you sent; but do they sell? I'm curious. In any event the frame-makers and guilders have profited by those you sent to me. (Haydn to Artaria, 20 July, 1781)

The Grand Duchess Maria Fedorowna took
lessons from Haydn during her stay in
Vienna in the winter of 1781–82. Some pieces
of Haydn's new string quartet cycle, which
the composer dedicated to the husband of
the Grand Duchess (and which later became
known under the name *Russian* Quartets,
Opus 33), were performed before the Russian
visitors. The six quartets, Opus 33 (Hoboken
III: 37–42), which Haydn completed in 1781
after nine years break from composing this
kind of music, were very important in his
stylistic development. The undisturbed work
of nine years spent in seclusion in the coun-
tryside matured his musical expression and
thematic approach, and these soon became
customary formulas in the musical language
of the day. A peculiarity of the cycle is the
scherzo, which replaced the minuet. From
this issues, after the *Russian* and *Jungfern*,
the third name of the cycle, *Gli Scherzi*.

156 GRAND DUCHESS
MARIA FEDOROWNA
(BORN DUCHESS
SOPHIE DOROTHEA)

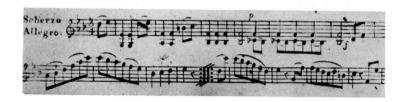

157–159 OPENING BARS OF
THREE SCHERZI FROM
ARTARIA'S FIRST EDITION
OF OPUS 33
(HOBOKEN III: 37–42)

160 GRAND DUKE PAVEL
PETROWICH (LATER
TSAR PAUL I OF RUSSIA,
1754–1801), TO WHOM
THE QUARTETS OPUS 33
WERE DEDICATED

161 TITLE-PAGE OF THE
QUARTETS OPUS 33, FROM
WHICH THEIR NAME THE
'JUNGFERN' [MAIDEN]
DERIVES

*As a great patron and connoisseur of music, I take the liberty of humbly offering Your*
*Serene Highness my brand new à quadro for two violins, viola [and] violoncello concertante*
*correctly copied, at a subscription price of 6 ducats. They are written in a new and special*
*way, for I have not composed any for 10 years. The noble subscribers who live abroad will*
*receive their copies before I issue them here. I beg for your favour, and a gracious acceptance*
*of your offer...* (Haydn, 3 December, 1781)

162 CHARLES III, KING
OF SPAIN (1716–1788),
WHO IN 1781 SENT TO
PRINCE ESTERHÁZY'S
FAMOUS COMPOSER A
GOLDEN SNUFF-BOX SET
WITH DIAMONDS

LUIGI BOCCHERINI

163 THE COMPOSER
LUIGI BOCCHERINI
(1743–1805), WHO WAS
THEN ACTIVE IN SPAIN,
WROTE TO HAYDN IN
1781 ASKING TO MAKE
HIS ACQUAINTANCE

*Palatium Principis Pauli Antonÿ ab Esterhasÿ de Galantha in platea, quae Wallerstrafs dicitur.*    *Das Majorat Hauß des Fürstens Paul Anthonÿ von Esterhaß de Galantha in der Waller Strasse.*

164 THE ESTERHÁZY
PALACE IN VIENNA
(IN THE WALLNER-
STRASSE), WHERE
HAYDN LIVED DURING
THE WINTER SEASON

165 JOSEPH HAYDN.
SILHOUETTE BY
HIERONYMUS
LÖSCHENKOHL (1785)

*Joseph Haydn*

Freemasonry, which gained more and more ground in educated circles during the reign of Emperor Joseph II, also aroused Haydn's interest. He became a member of the 'For True Harmony' lodge on the 11th February, 1785, but the spiritual content of this movement had no effect on his art. He was nominated for admission to the lodge by the Hungarian aristocrat Count Anton Apponyi and by the Viennese court secretary, Franz Philipp von Weber. He had written to the latter as follows:

*Nobly born,*
*Most highly respected Herr Hoff Secretaire,*
*The highly advantageous impression which Freemasonry has made on me has long awakened in my breast the sincerest wish to become a member of the Order, with its humanitarian and wise principles. I turn to you, Sir, with the most urgent request that you have the great kindness to intervene on my behalf with the Lodge of the Order, to implement this my petition, as indicated above.*
*I have the honour to remain, with profound esteem,*

*Your obedient servant,*
*Josephus Haydn,*
*CapellMeister to Prince Esterházy.*

*Vienna, the 29th of the Christmas Month, 1784.*

JOHANN VANHAL

Carolus Ditters a Dittersdorf
Nomenque erit indelebile
Ovid: Metamorph. Lib.XV. v.878

Mr. MICHAEL KELLY.
Engraved
By Neagle from a painting by Laurence.

168 KARL DITTERS VON
DITTERSDORF (1739–1799)

169 THE IRISH SINGER
MICHAEL KELLY
(1762–1826) WAS PRESENT
WHEN DITTERSDORF,
HAYDN, MOZART AND
VANHALL IN VIENNA
PLAYED A QUARTET
WITH PAISIELLO
IN THE AUDIENCE

*Once when Haydn was going through the streets in Vienna with Dittersdorf, they heard some Haydn minuets being very badly played in a tavern. 'We ought to have some fun with these bunglers,' said one to the other. They went into the tavern, ordered a glass, and listened a while. 'Who wrote these minuets anyway?' Haydn finally asked. They gave him his own name. 'Ach, that's pretty miserable stuff!' he exclaimed. At this the musicians flew into such a rage that one of them would have broken his violin on Haydn's head, if he had not speedily taken flight.* (Griesinger)

Dignum laude virum Musa vetat mori.
Horst.

170 (Left) Wolfgang
Amadeus Mozart
(1756–1791)

171 (Right)
Leopold Mozart
(1719–1787)

In the period from December 1782 to
January 1785—an unusually long time
for him—Mozart composed a series of
six string quartets (K. 387, 421, 428,
458, 464, 465). As he had taken Haydn's
chamber music for his model, he dedicated the cycle to Haydn.

*I tell you, as God's my witness, and as an
honest man, that your son is the greatest
composer I know, personally or by reputation: he has taste, and above all, the
greatest possible knowledge of composition.* (Haydn about Mozart, from a letter
to Leopold Mozart, 16 February, 1785)

172 Schulerstrasse
in Vienna. Mozart's
apartment with
projecting bay

173 THE GRABEN,
VIENNA, WHERE MOZART LIVED
1781–1782
AND 1784

174 MOZART'S DEDICATION
OF HIS SIX STRING
QUARTETS TO HAYDN

*Al mio caro Amico Haydn*

*Un Padre, avendo risolto di mandare i suoi figli nel gran
Mondo, stimò doverli affidare alla protezione, e condotta
d'un Uomo molto celebre in allora, il quale per buona sorte,
era di più il suo migliore Amico.—Eccoti dunque del pari,
Uom celebr, ed Amico mio carissimo i sei miei figli.—Essi sono,
è vero il frutto di una lunga, e laboriosa fatica, pur la speranza
fattami da più Amici di vederla almeno in parte compensata,
m'incoraggisce, e mi lusinga, che questi parti siano per esermi
un giorno di qualche consolazione.—Tu stesso Amico carissimo,
nell'ultimo tuo Soggiorno in questa Capitale, me ne dimostrasti
la tua soddisfazione.—Questo tuo suffragio mi anima sopra
tutto, perché Io te li raccommandi, e mi fa sperare, che non ti
sembreranno del tutto indegni del tuo favore.—Piacciati dunque
accoglierli benignamente, ed esser loro Padre, Guida, ed Amico!
Da questo momento, Io ti cedo i miei diritti sopra di essi: ti
supplico però di guardare con indulgenza i difetti, che l'occhio
parziale di Padre mi può aver celati, e di continuar loro
malgrado, la generosa tua Amicizia a chi tanto l'apprezza,
mentre sono di tutto Cuore.*

*Amico Carissimo*
*Vienna il p.mo Settembre 1785.*

*il tuo Sincerissimo Amico*
*W. A. Mozart*

*To my dear friend Haydn*

*A father, having resolved to send his sons into the great
world, finds it advisable to entrust them to the protection
and guidance of a highly celebrated man, the more so since
this man, by a stroke of luck, is his best friend. Here,
then, celebrated man and dearest friend, are my six sons.
Truly, they are the fruit of a long and laborious effort, but
the hope, strengthened by several of my friends, that this
effort would, at least in some small measure, be rewarded,
encourages and comforts me that one day these children
may be a source of consolation to me. You yourself, dearest friend, during your last sojourn in this capital, expressed to me your satisfaction with these works. Your approval encourages me more than anything else, and thus I
entrust them to your care, and hope that they are not wholly
unworthy of your favour. Do but receive them kindly, and
be their father, guide and friend! From this moment I cede
to you all my rights over them: I pray you to be indulgent
towards their faults, which a father's partial eye may have
overlooked, and despite them, to cloak them in the mantle
of your generosity which I value so highly. From the bottom of my heart, I am, dearest friend,*

*Your most sincere friend,*
*W. A. Mozart*
*Vienna, 1st September, 1785.*

91

175 Joseph Haydn.
Life-sized painting
by Christian Ludwig
Seehas (1785)

176 Franz Georg Edler
von Kees, a Viennese
music lover

177 Maria Wilhelmine,
Countess von Thun,
born Ulfeld (1744–1800),
one of the leading
personalities of the
musical salons in
Vienna

Since a new contract made on the 1st of January 1779, Haydn was no longer bound, even formally. He could at last dispose of his own compositions. Therefore most of his works were no longer composed for the Esterházy palace, and no restrictions were put on his making business arrangements about them. (As a compensation, and also as a friendly gesture, Haydn dedicated some compositions to members of the Prince's family and published them thus.) From 1780 on, Haydn exchanged regular correspondence with the music publishing house of Artaria in Vienna. The piano sonatas, songs and pieces of chamber music published by Artaria were the first works which brought him monetary profit. Moreover, at last Haydn had the chance of checking his published works to see whether the texts were true to the original and to make corrections. By this time, in addition to Artaria, several other publishers made efforts to obtain Haydn's works: Boyer in Paris, Torricella in Vienna, Forster in London, and Breitkopf in Leipzig, among others.

180 An Artaria edition
(1781) of Haydn's
Divertimenti

181 Gideon Ernst von
Loudon (Laudon,
1717[sic]–1790), the
famous Austrian
Field Marshall

*I send you herewith the Symphony, Sir, which was so full of mistakes that the fellow who wrote it ought to have his paw chopped off. The last or 4th movement is not practicable for the pianoforte, and I don't think it necessary to include it in print: the word 'Laudon' will contribute more to the sale than any ten finales. My continued unhappy condition, that is, the present necessity to operate a polyphus on my nose, made it impossible for me to work up to now. You must therefore have patience about the* Lieder, *for another week, or at most a fortnight, until my enfeebled head, with God's help, regains its former vigour. Please have the goodness to present my respects to Count Durazzo, and tell him that I cannot remember the themes of the trios nor can I recall having received them. I searched carefully all through my music and papers, and could find no trace of them; if it pleases the Count, however, I shall send him a catalogue of all my trios. I await the favour of your reply and remain, Sir, most respectfully, . . .*(Haydn to Artaria, Esterháza, 8 April, 1783)

*His Majesty, King of Prussia, etc., etc. is sensible of the mark of respect which* Herr Kapellmeister *Haydn, in sending him six new Symphonies, again wishes to show to His Serene Majesty. They have especially pleased him, and there is no doubt that His Highness has always appreciated* Herr Kapellmeister *Haydn's works, and will appreciate them at all times. To provide concrete assurance of the same, he sends him the enclosed ring as a mark of His Highness' satisfaction and of the favour in which he holds him.*
*Potsdam, 21st April, 1787.* F. Wilhelm.
(Friedrich Wilhelm II to Haydn)

The six *Prussian* Quartets (Opus 50, Hoboken III: 44–49, 1787) and the six of the first *Tost* series of quartets (Opus 54–55, Hoboken III: 57–62, from around 1788 approximately) indicated a new stage in the development, now slowing down, of Haydn's style. The time of 'discoveries' was over. In the period which followed, he was to work on refining the basic elements of his melody, harmony and timbre.

182 FRIEDRICH WILHELM II, KING OF PRUSSIA (1744–1797)

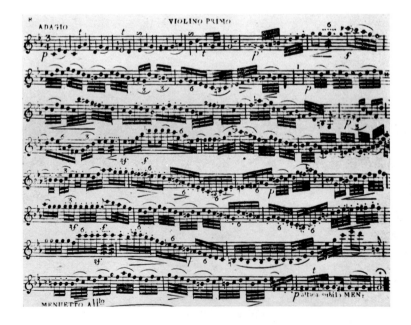

183 THE DELICATE, FLEETING, SEEMINGLY IMPROMPTU MELODY OF THE FIRST VIOLIN FROM THE ADAGIO OF THE C-MINOR QUARTET (HOBOKEN III: 57)

184 KRAFT ERNST,
PRINCE VON
OETTINGEN-WALLERSTEIN

185 COUNT CLAUDE
FRANÇOIS MARIE D'OGNY

In 1786, the musical society of Paris, 'Les Concerts de la Loge Olympique', ordered symphonies from Haydn through the good offices of the Count d'Ogny, as did the South-German Prince von Oettingen-Wallerstein in 1788.

*...Since I am sure that Your Grace takes an interest in all my doings (far more, in fact, than I deserve), I should like to tell Your Grace that last week I received a present of a charming gold snuff-box, weighing the value of 34 ducats, from Prince Oetting von Wallerstein, together with an invitation to pay him a visit at his expense sometime this year; His Highness is especially desirous of making my personal acquaintance (a pleasant encouragement for my drooping spirits). Whether I shall make up my mind to go is another question...* (Haydn to Frau von Genzinger, 14 March, 1790)

186 Don José Alvarez
de Toledo y Gonzaga,
a painting by Goya.
On the cover of the
music: 'Del Sr. Haydn'

That Haydn's music was also known and loved in Spain is shown by the commission
from Cadiz in 1785 for an orchestral composition to illustrate in music the seven words
of Christ on the Cross. *(The Seven Words)*

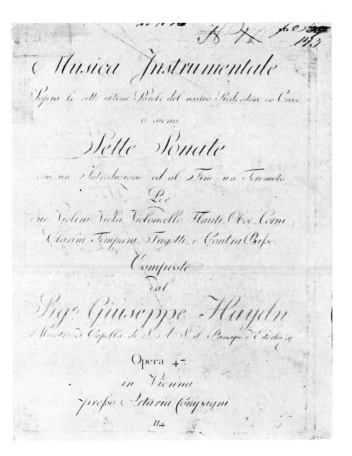

187–188 Frontispiece
and beginning of the
Sonata No. VII from
the first Viennese
Artaria edition of
'The Seven Words'
(Hoboken XX/I)

*Long in Madrid thy works, with beauties fraught,*
*Of censors grave have so engrossed the thought,*
*Prizes have been bestowed—so great their zeal,*
*Of those who best thy labours, study, feel.—*
*While, where the Manzanares winds her stream,*
*So much art thou her honour [sic] glory, theme,*
*Her nymphs with fadeless wreaths thy brows entwine,*
*As tho' Spain birth had given to worth like thine.*

(From the section referring to Haydn in the poem 'La
Música', written by Don Tomas de Yriarte in 1779)

*It was approximately fifteen years ago that I was asked by a canon of Cadiz to prepare*
*instrumental music to the seven words of Jesus on the Cross. It was customary then to*
*present an oratorio every year during Lent in the cathedral of Cadiz. The following arrange-*
*ments must have contributed to the dramatic effect considerably: that is to say, the walls, win-*
*dows and pillars of the church were covered with black cloth, and only a large lamp hanging*
*in the centre lit the holy darkness. At noon, all doors were closed; and then the music began.*
*After a suitable overture the bishop mounted the pulpit, pronounced one of the seven words,*
*and gave a sermon on it. As soon as this was over, he left the pulpit and knelt in front of*
*the altar. This interval was filled with music. The bishop mounted and left the pulpit a*
*second time, then a third, and so on, and each time the orchestra recommenced after the oration*
*ended. My composition had to be adapted to this presentation. The task to make seven adagios,*
*each of ten minutes, follow one another without tiring the listener, was not an easy one; and*
*I soon found myself unable to stick to the prescribed time. The music had originally no text,*
*and was also printed without any . . .* (Vienna, March 1801, Haydn).

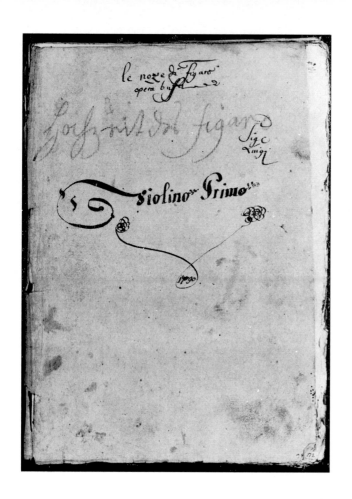

189 (LEFT) TITLE-PAGE
OF A PART COPY MADE
IN ESZTERHÁZA OF
MOZART'S
'LE NOZZE DI FIGARO'
(K. 492)

190 (RIGHT) JOSEPH
HAYDN. AN ANONYMOUS
SILHOUETTE, PROBABLY
FROM THE END OF
THE 1780S

In 1789, Haydn procured the score of Mozart's *Le nozze di Figaro* for the Eszterháza ensemble. The parts were copied, but, since the Prince had died in the meantime and the orchestra was dissolved, the performance planned for 1790 never took place.

*You ask me for an* opera buffa. *Most willingly, if you want to have one of my vocal compositions for yourself alone. But if you intend to produce it on the stage in Prague, in that case I cannot comply with your wish, because all my operas are far too closely connected with our personal circle (Esterház, in Hungary), and moreover they would not produce the proper effect, which I calculated in accordance with the locality. It would be quite another matter if I were to have the great good fortune to compose a brand new libretto for your theatre. But even then I should be risking a good deal, for scarcely any man can brook comparison with the great Mozart.*

*If I could only impress on the soul of every friend of music, and on high personages in particular, how inimitable are Mozart's works, how profound, how musically intelligent, how extraordinarily sensitive! (for this is how I understand them, how I feel them)—why then the nations would vie with each other to possess such a jewel within their frontiers. Prague should hold him fast—but should reward him, too; for without this, the history of great geniuses is sad indeed, and gives but little encouragement to posterity to further exertions; and unfortunately this is why so many promising intellects fall by the wayside. It enrages me to think that this incomparable Mozart is not yet engaged by some imperial or royal court! Forgive me if I lose my head, but I love the man so dearly...*
(Haydn to *Oberverpflegs-Verwalter* Franz Rott, Prague, 1787)

191 THE SCHOTTENKIRCHE
AT THE SCHOTTENHOF,
IN VIENNA

192 MANUSCRIPT OF WHAT
WAS PROBABLY THE FIRST
LETTER FROM FRAU VON
GENZINGER TO HAYDN

*Most respected Herr v. Hayden,*
*With your kind permission, I take the liberty of sending you a pianoforte arrangement of the beautiful Andante from your so admirable composition. I made this arrangement from the score quite by myself, without the least help from my teacher; please be good enough to correct any mistakes you may find in it. I hope that you are enjoying perfect health, and I wish for nothing more than to see you soon again in Vienna, so that I may demonstrate still further the esteem in which I hold you. I remain, in true friendship,*

*Your obedient servant,*
*Maria Anna Noble v. Gennzinger*
*née Noble v. Kayser.*
*My husband and children also ask me to send you their kindest regards.*
*Vienna, 10th June 1789.*

The first exchange of letters between Haydn and Marianne von Genzinger, who was 23 years younger, took place in the summer of 1789. The physician, Dr. Leopold von Genzinger, played an important part in Vienna's musical life. The moving spirit of the musical gatherings at the house of the art-loving physician was his unusually well-educated wife. No portrait of her has survived, but the magic of her personality speaks from Haydn's letters.

The relationship between Haydn and Frau von Genzinger was entirely different from the love that Luigia Polzelli had been able to offer him. Music united them in honest, but reserved, friendship. Their first letters already spoke of music: namely, Frau von Genzinger was practising with great care a piano arrangement of the slow movement of a Haydn symphony. The intimacy of the hours spent with her, in a state of tranquil happiness, made it easier for Haydn to suffer the months at Eszterháza, which were becoming less and less bearable.

*Nobly born,*
*Most highly respected and kindest Frau von Gennzinger,*
*Well, here I sit in my wilderness—forsaken—like a poor waif—almost without any human society—melancholy—full of the memories of past glorious days—yes! past alas!—and who knows when these days shall return again? Those wonderful parties? Where the whole circle is one heart, one soul—all these beautiful musical evenings—it can only be remembered, and not described—where are all these enthusiastic moments?—all gone—and gone for a long time. Your Grace mustn't be surprised that I haven't written up to now to thank you. I found everything at home in confusion, and for 3 days I did not know if I was Capell-master or Capell-servant. Nothing could console me, my whole house was in confusion, my pianoforte which I usually love so much was perverse and disobedient, it irritated rather than calmed me, I could only sleep very little, even my dreams persecuted me; and then, just when I was happily dreaming that I was listening to the opera,* Le Nozze di Figaro, *that horrible North wind woke me and almost blew my nightcap off my head; I lost 20 lbs. in weight in 3 days, for the good Viennese food I had in me disappeared on the journey... Forgive me, kindest and most gracious lady, for filling the very first letter with such stupid nonsense, and for killing time with such a wretched scrawl, but you must forgive a man whom the Viennese terribly spoiled. I am gradually getting used to country life, however, and yesterday I studied for the first time, and quite Haydnish, too...* (Haydn to Frau von Genzinger, Eszterháza, 9 February, 1790)

*Nobly born,*
*Most esteemed and kindest Frau von Gennzinger!*
*I ask Your Grace's forgiveness a million times for having so long delayed the answer to your*
*kind 2 letters. This is not negligence (a sin from which Heaven will preserve me as long as*
*I live) but is because of the many things I have to do for my most gracious Prince in his*
*present most melancholy condition. The death of his wife so crushed the Prince that we had*
*to use every means in our power to pull His Highness out of his depression, and thus the*
*first 3 days I arranged enlarged chamber music every evening with no singing; but the poor*
*Prince, during the concert of the first evening, became so depressed when he heard my favourite*
*Adagio in D that we had quite a time to brighten his mood with the other pieces.*
*On the 4th day we had an opera, on the 5th a comedy, and then our theatre daily as usual.*
*Meanwhile I ordered them to prepare the old opera* L'amor Artigiano *by Gasman, because*
*the Prince had said to me recently that he would like to see it: I wrote 3 new arias for it,*
*which I shall be sending Your Grace shortly, not because of their beauty but to show Your*
*Grace how diligent I am. Your Grace shall receive the promised Symphony during the*
*month of April, but in time so that it can be produced at the Kees Concert.* (Haydn to Frau
von Genzinger, 14 March, 1790)

195 From the
manuscript of the
Sonata in E flat major
(Hoboken XVI: 49)

*...This Sonata is in E flat, brand new, and was written especially for Your Grace to be hers forever, but it is a curious coincidence that the last movement is the very same Minuet and Trio which Your Grace asked me for in your last letter. This Sonata was destined for Your Grace a year ago, and only the Adagio is quite new, and I especially recommend this movement to your attention, for it contains many things which I shall analyse for Your Grace when the time comes; it is rather difficult but full of feeling...*

*...It's only a pity that Your Grace doesn't own a Schantz fortepiano, on which everything is better expressed. I thought that Your Grace might turn over your still tolerable harpsichord to Fräulein Peperl, and buy a new fortepiano for yourself. Your beautiful hands and their facility of execution deserve this and much more. I know I ought to have composed this Sonata in accordance with the capabilities of your clavier, but I found this impossible because I was no longer accustomed to it.* (Haydn to Frau von Genzinger, 20 and 27 June, 1790)

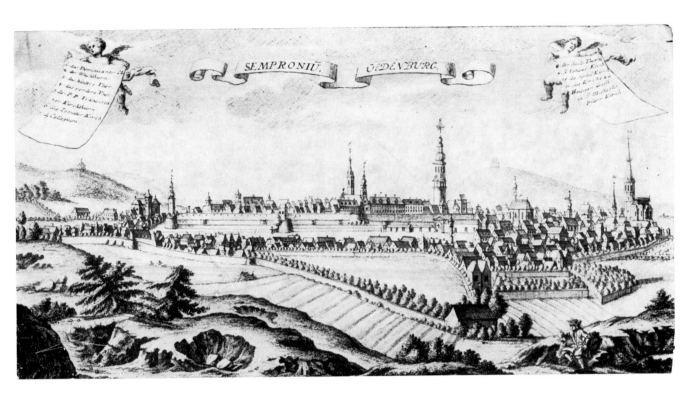

197 VIEW OF THE CITY
OF SOPRON (OEDENBURG).
THE JANITOR OF THE
ESTERHÁZY PALACE IN
SOPRON FORWARDED
HAYDN'S CORRESPONDENCE
TO AND FROM VIENNA

198 HAYDN c. 1788.
AN ANONYMOUS MINIATURE,
WATERCOLOUR ON IVORY

*I was astonished to see from your kind letter that Your Grace did not receive my last letter . . . this is not the first time that some of my letters, and also those of many others, have gone astray, inasmuch as our letter-bag, on its way to Oedenburg, is always opened by the housemaster there (in order to put the letters into it), as a result of which mistakes and other disagreeable occurrences have often arisen . . . Anyway, these curious people, male or female, cannot have discovered anything improper in this last letter, or in any of the others either . . . Your Grace therefore mustn't be angry at your Haydn who, often as his Prince absents himself from Estoras, cannot go to Vienna even for 24 hours; it's scarcely credible, and yet the refusal is always couched in such polite terms, so polite in fact that I just don't have the heart to insist on receiving the permission . . . Again I find that I am forced to remain here. Your Grace can imagine how much I lose by having to do so. It really is sad always to be a slave, but Providence wills it so. I'm a poor creature! Always plagued by hard work, very few hours of recreation, and friends? What am I saying? One true one? There aren't any true friends any more—one lady friend? Oh yes! There might be one. But she's far away from me.* (Haydn to Frau von Genzinger, 13 and 30 May, 27 June, 1790)

Monatgagequittung

| Nr. | | Namen |
|---|---|---|
| 1 | Kapellmeister | Haydn |
| 2 | Sängerin | Bologna |
| 3 | do | Sassi |
| 4 | mit ihrem Manne | Polzelli |
| 5 | do | Benvenutti |
| 6 | do | Zecchielli |
| 7 | do | Melo |
| 8 | Sänger | Braghetti |
| 9 | do | Prizzi |
| 10 | do | Paoli |
| 11 | do | Martinelli |
| 12 | do | Majeroni |
| 13 | do | Amici |
| 14 | do | Ungericht |
| 15 | do | Specht |
| 16 | Violinista | Tomasini |
| 17 | do | Tost |
| 18 | do | Purksteiner |
| 19 | do | Leop. Hirsch |
| 20 | do | Fux |
| 21 | do | Oliva |
| 22 | do mit ihm | Polzelli |
| 23 | Violoncellista | Kraft |
| 24 | do | Tauber |
| 25 | Violonista | Jean Dietzl |
| 26 | Waldhornista | Oliva |
| 27 | do | Pauer |
| 28 | do | Nickl |
| 29 | do | Jos. Dietzl |
| 30 | Hautboista | Fr. Czervenka |
| 31 | do | Mayer |
| 32 | Flautroversista | Hirsch |
| 33 | do | Schiringer |
| 34 | Fagotista | Czervenka |
| 35 | do | Peczival |
| 36 | do | Steiner |
| 37 | Garderobba | Porta |
| 38 | Copista | Schillinger |

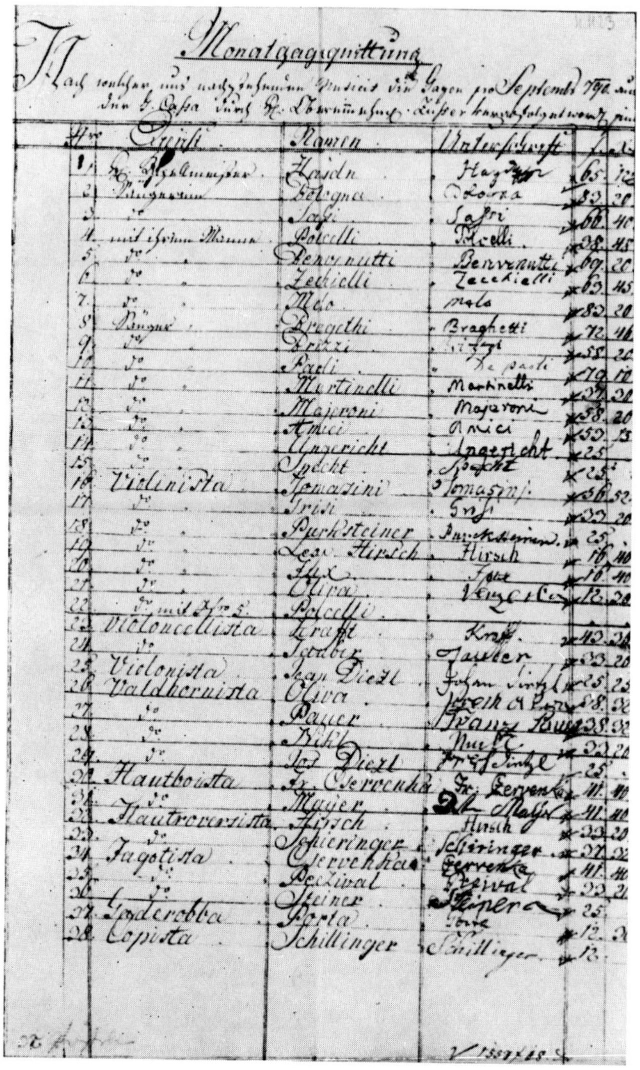

199 THE LAST PAYROLL OF THE OPERA COMPANY BEFORE THE ORCHESTRA WAS DISBANDED

On the 28th September 1790, Prince Nikolaus Esterházy quite unexpectedly died. This meant the end of musical life in Eszterháza. The heir, Prince Anton, disbanded the orchestra and left the residence. Haydn was assured of the continuation of his salary, but he left Eszterháza as if escaping, and moved to Vienna.

# THE INDEPENDENT ARTIST (1791–1795)

200 VIENNA. VIEW FROM
THE KAUNITZ PALACE.
PAINTING BY
BERNARDO BELLOTTO

201 Vienna. View with
the Karlskirche, the
Belvedere and the
Schwarzenberg Palace

*Salomon, a native of Cologne and formerly engaged as violinist by Prince Henry of Prussia, had oftentimes written to Haydn from London to urge on him a journey to England. Haydn always answered that so long as his Prince was alive, he could not leave him. Prince Nikolaus Esterházy died on September 28, 1790, at a time when Gallini had gone to Italy for singers and to recruit among others the celebrated Davide for his London Professional Concerts in Hanover Square. Salomon himself was in Cologne on his way back to London after he had engaged several German musicians for Gallini. As soon as he heard of the death of Prince Esterházy, he hurried to Vienna. Toward evening someone knocked at Haydn's room; Salomon walked in, and his first words were, 'Get ready to travel. In a fortnight, we go together to London.' Haydn began by resisting the proposal. He pointed to his ignorance of the English language and to his inexperience in travel. These objections, however, were soon put aside.* (Griesinger)

202 (Left)
Johann Peter Salomon
(1745–1815)

203 (Right) Wolfgang
Amadeus Mozart

*Prince Anton readily granted permission for the journey at once, but it was not all right as far as Haydn's friends were concerned, the ones who had so often before tried to persuade him to leave Vienna. They reminded him of his age (sixty years), of the discomforts of a long journey, and of many other things to shake his resolve. But in vain! Mozart especially took pains to say, 'Papa!' as he usually called him, 'you have had no training for the great world, and you speak too few languages.'—'Oh!' replied Haydn, 'my language is understood all over the world.'* (Dies)

*Mozart said to Haydn, at a happy meal with Salomon, 'You will not bear it very long and will probably soon come back again, because you are no longer young.' 'But I am still vigorous and in good health,' answered Haydn.* (Griesinger)

204 (Left) Ferdinand II,
King of the two
Sicilies (1751–1825)

205 (Right) Prince
Anton III Grassalkovich

*The discharged musicians sought and easily found further prosperity; it was a big recom-
mendation for them to have perfected themselves under Haydn's direction. Haydn himself
was approached on behalf of Count Grassalkovics about entering his service as Kapellmeister. On this occasion, however, he showed his attachment to his Prince and turned the
proposal down... (Dies)*

*Shortly before his departure, Haydn took to King Ferdinand of Naples, who was in Vienna
at that time, several works that he had commissioned. 'The day after tomorrow we will perform them,' said the King. 'I am eternally sorry,' Haydn replied, 'that I cannot be present,
because the day after tomorrow I leave for England.' 'What? and you have promised me to
come to Naples?' The King left the room rather indignantly and only came back an hour
later. Haydn had to promise him again to make a journey to Naples after his return from
England. He received a letter of introduction to the King's envoy in London, Prince Castelcicala, and the King sent after him a valuable snuff-box. (Griesinger)*

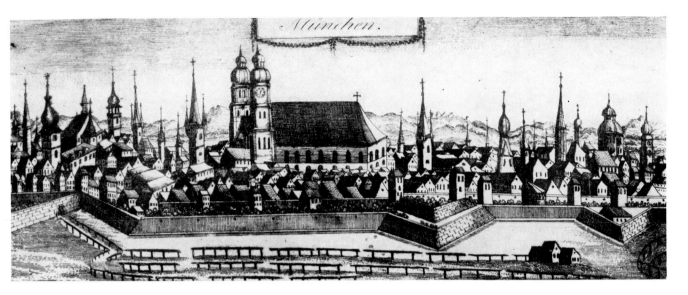

206 MUNICH

Griesinger reports that 'Haydn set out on his journey with Salomon on December 15, 1790.' Their journey to Calais took them through Germany and Belgium (they avoided Paris, because Haydn feared the street fighting, and Salomon also feared the competition in Paris, and the latter therefore prescribed a quick pace). Their first stop was Munich, where Haydn made the acquaintance of Christian Cannabich.

207 CHRISTIAN CANNABICH
(1731–1798)

208 KRAFT ERNST
PRINCE VON
OETTINGEN-WALLERSTEIN,
WHOM HAYDN MET
AT WALLERSTEIN IN
DECEMBER 1790

209 ELECTOR
MAXIMILIAN FRANZ
(1756–1801)

*In the capital, Bonn, he was surprised in more ways than one . . . Salomon took Haydn to the court chapel to hear Mass. Hardly had they entered the church and found themselves a good place, when the High Mass began. The first sounds announced a work of Haydn's. Our Haydn supposed it as a coincidence that was so obliging as to flatter him, but it was very pleasant to him to hear his own work. Toward the end of Mass, someone approached and invited him to go into the oratory, where he was expected. Haydn went there and was no little astonished to see that the Elector Maximilian had summoned him there, took him immediately by the hand, and presented to him his musicians with the words, 'Thus I make you acquainted with your much-cherished Haydn.'* (Dies)

210 LONDON BRIDGE

The fifty-nine-year-old Haydn reached the English Channel at the beginning of January 1791, after a troublesome journey full of incidents.

*Most noble Prince of the Holy Roman Empire!*
*I report respectfully that, despite unpleasant weather and a great many bad roads throughout the whole trip, I arrived in London this 2nd of January, happy and in good health. My arrival created a great stir, and forced me to take larger quarters that same evening: I received so many calls that I shall hardly be able to repay them in 6 weeks. Both the ambassadors, i.e. Prince Castelcicala of Naples and Herr Baron von Stadion; and I had the pleasure of lunching with both of them at 6 o'clock in the evening... (Haydn to Prince Anton Ester-házy, London, 8 January, 1791)*

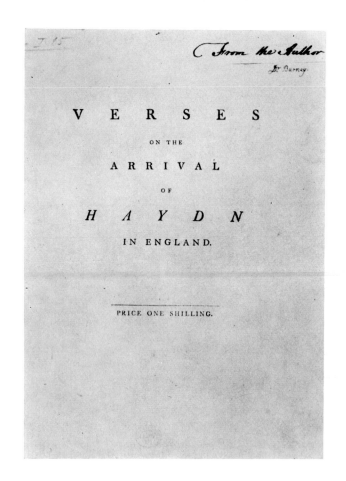

Players as seldom have been known to write
As Generals, who plan, in ranks to fight.
SHAKSPEAR, *in execution, could at most
But feebly represent his Hamlet's ghost;
But by his wond'rous pen's immortal aid,
All the great Actors of our stage were made:
Our Bettertons and Booths, our Wilks and Quin,
And all Thalia's laughter-loving kin.
GARRICK, with comic sport, and tragic rage,
Taught Shakspear's self to please a distant age;
With eye and voice, with gesture and with feature,
He best interpreted both him and Nature.
A Proteus in his art, who seem'd design'd
To be the Index of all human kind.*

HAYDN! *Great Sovereign of the tuneful art!
Thy works alone supply an ample chart
Of all the mountains, seas, and fertile plains,
Within the compass of its wide domains.—
Is there an Artist of the present day
Untaught by thee to think, as well as play?
Whose head thy science has not well supplied?
Whose hand thy labours have not fortified?—*

Old rules geographic soon were out of date,
When the terrestrial sphere was found oblate:
When wise Copernicus the orbs arrang'd,
The system of Astronomy was chang'd:
And now no laws of harmony are found,
No treatise, code, or theory of sound,

Whose narrow limits, fixt by pedants vain,
Thy bold creative genius can restrain.
IMAGINATION, *which, like garden bird,
Was long forbid the skies, by rules absurd,
Has now broke loose—now takes her airy flight
To explore new worlds, and regions of delight.*

Thy style has gain'd disciples, converts, friends,
As far as Music's thrilling power extends.
Nor has great Newton more to satisfaction
Demonstrated the influence of Attraction.
And though to Italy of right belong
The undisputed sovereignty of Song;
Yet ev'ry nation of the earth must now
To Germany pre-eminence allow
For instrumental *powers, unknown before
Thy happy flights had taught her sons to soar.*

Welcome, great Master! to our favour'd Isle,
Already partial to thy name and style;
Long may thy fountain of Invention run
In streams as rapid as it first begun;
While skill for each fantastic whim provides,
And certain science ev'ry current guides!

Oh, may thy days, from human sufferings free,
Be blest with glory and felicity!
With full fruition, to a distant hour,
Of all thy magic and creative pow'r!
Blest in thyself, with rectitude of mind;
And blessing, with thy talents, all mankind!

211–212 VERSES ON THE
ARRIVAL OF HAYDN BY
DR. BURNEY

213 HANOVER
SQUARE ROOMS

*My arrival caused a great sensation throughout the whole city, and I went the round of all the newspapers for 3 successive days. Everybody wants to know me. I had to dine out 6 times up to now, and if I wanted, I could dine out every day; but first I must consider my health, and 2nd my work. Except for the nobility, I admit no callers till 2 o'clock in the afternoon . . . Yesterday I was invited to a grand amateur concert, but I arrived a bit late, and when I showed my ticket they wouldn't let me in but led me to an antichamber, where I had to wait till the piece which was then being played in the hall was over. Then they opened the door, and I was conducted, on the arm of the* entrepreneur, *up to the centre of the hall to the front of the orchestra, amid universal applause, and there I was stared at and greeted by a great number of English compliments. I was assured that such honours have not been conferred on anyone for 50 years . . .* (Haydn to Frau von Genzinger, 8 January, 1791)

On the 11th March 1791 the orchestra assembled by Salomon and conducted by Joseph Haydn performed for the first time at the famous concert hall in Hanover Square and played the Symphony in D major (Hoboken I: 96).

*The first Concert under the auspices of* HAYDN *was last night, and never, perhaps, was there a richer musical treat. It is not wonderful that to souls capable of being touched by music,* HAYDN *should be an object of homage, and even of idolatry; for like our own* SHAKSPEARE, *he moves and governs the passions at his will. His* new Grand Overture *was pronounced by every scientific ear to be a most wonderful composition; but the first movement in particular rises in grandeur of subject, and in the rich variety of* air *and passion, beyond any even of his own productions . . . We were happy to see the Concert so well attended the first Night; for we cannot suppress our very anxious hopes, that the first musical genius of the age may be induced, by our liberal welcome, to take up his residence in England.* (Morning Chronicle)

214 Haydn in 1791.
Engraving by
Francesco Bartolozzi
after a lost miniature
by M. A. Ott

215 Charles Burney
(1726–1814). Engraving
by Francesco Bartolozzi

116

216 Chelsea Hospital;
Burney worked in
the district of
Chelsea at the time
of his friendship
with Haydn

217 The engraver
Francesco Bartolozzi,
friend and portrait
painter of Haydn

117

218 OXFORD

219 WILLIAM PITT THE
YOUNGER

*On 5th Nov. I was guest at a lunch given in honour of the Lord Mayor. The new Lord Mayor and his wife ate at the first table No. 1, then the Lord Chanceler and both the Scherifs, Duc de Lids [Leeds], Minister Pitt and the other judges of the first rank... No toast was more applauded than that to Mr. Pitt.* (From Haydn's First London Notebook)

220 QUEEN'S COLLEGE,
OXFORD

221 FRANZ JOSEPH CLEMENT
(1780–1842), ONE OF
THE PERFORMERS AT THE
CONCERT ARRANGED IN
HAYDN'S HONOUR

F. J. Clement
de Vienne
Virtuoso du Violon
à l'age de 8 ans.

Henri Reyfell 1789

## HAYDN'S HONORARY DEGREE AT OXFORD

Due to the good offices of Dr. Burney, Oxford University conferred an honorary degree on Haydn, on the 8th July 1791. It was then that the Symphony, in G major (Hoboken I: 92), which Haydn had composed in Eszterháza, but which has become generally known as the *Oxford* Symphony, was performed for the first time in England. After his impoverished childhood and years of hard service Haydn was extraordinarily proud of this honour; to the end of his life he set a great value on this Doctorate.

*I had to pay 1½ guineas for having the bells rung at Oxforth [sic] in connection with my doctor's degree, and ½ a guinea for the robe. The trip cost 6 guineas.* (From Haydn's Second London Notebook)

119

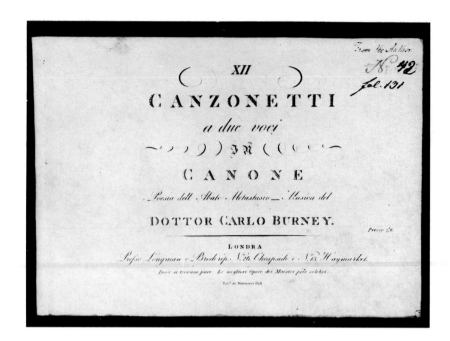

222–223 TITLE-PAGES
OF WORKS BY
CHARLES BURNEY AND
A. CAMPBELL DEDICATED
TO HAYDN (FROM
HAYDN'S LIBRARY)

224 HANDEL MEMORIAL
CONCERT IN
WESTMINSTER ABBEY

In May 1791 Haydn attended the Handel Concerts in Westminster Abbey, which had become a tradition of some years' standing. More than a thousand musicians participated in the performance of the oratorios. (Haydn attended the performances of *Israel in Egypt* and *Messiah* and heard parts of *Esther*, *Saul* and *Judas Maccabaeus* too.) Haydn said: 'He is the master of us all.'

*8 days before Pentecost I heard 4,000 charity children in St. Paul's Church sing the song noted below. One performer indicated the tempo. No music ever moved me so deeply in my whole life as this devotional and innocent music.*

*N. B. All the children are newly clad, and enter in procession. The organist first played the melody very nicely and simply, and then they all began to sing at once.* (From Haydn's First London Notebook)

*A gang of rowdy fellows sang this song with all their might. They yelled so loudly that you could hear them 1,000 paces away from the street, in every nook and cranny.* (From Haydn's Second London Notebook)

226 Vauxhall Gardens
in London, the scene
of large public
festivities

227 Monument to
George Friedrich
Handel, by
L. R. Roubiliac (1738),
a copy of which stood
in Vauxhall Gardens

*Today, 4th June 1792, I was in Vauxhall where the King's birthday is celebrated. Over 30,000 lamps were burning, but because of the severe cold there were very few people present. The grounds and its variety are perhaps unique in the world. There are 155 little dining booths in various places, most charmingly situated, each comfortably seating 6 persons. There are very large alleys of trees, which form a wonderful roof above, and are magnificently illuminated. Tea, coffee and milk with almonds all cost nothing. The entrance fee is half a crown per person. The music is fairly good. A stone statue of Handel has been erected. On the 2nd inst. there was a masked ball, and on this evening they took in 3,000 guineas.*
(From Haydn's First London Notebook)

228 PORTRAIT OF HAYDN,
OIL PAINTING BY LUDWIG
GUTTENBRUNN, FROM
THE TIME OF HIS FIRST
STAY IN LONDON
(VERSION A)

*I asked him once in jest whether it was true that he had composed the Andante from the Drum Stroke [Symphony No. 94] to waken the English who fell asleep at his concert. 'No,' came the answer, 'but I was interested in surprising the public with something new, and in making a brilliant debut, so that my student Pleyel, who was at that time engaged with an orchestra in London (in 1792) and whose concerts had opened a week before mine, should not outdo me. The first Allegro of my symphony had already met with countless Bravos, but the enthusiasm reached its highest peak at the Andante with the Drum Stroke. Encore! Encore! sounded in every throat, and Pleyel himself complimented me on my idea.'* (Griesinger)

*When Haydn appeared in the orchestra and sat down at the pianoforte to direct a symphony himself, the curious audience in the parterre left their seats and crowded toward the orchestra the better to see the famous Haydn quite close. The seats in the middle of the floor were thus empty, and hardly were they empty when the great chandelier crashed down and broke into bits, throwing the numerous gathering into the greatest consternation. As soon as the first moment of fright was over and those who had pressed forward could think of the danger they had luckily escaped and find words to express it, several persons uttered the state of their feelings with loud cries of 'Miracle! Miracle!' Haydn himself was deeply moved and thanked merciful Providence that had thus allowed him in a certain way to be the cause for or the means of saving the lives of at least thirty people. (Dies)*

230 HAYMARKET
OPERA-HOUSE

Gallini, the manager of the King's Theatre (Haymarket), which was under the patronage of the Prince of Wales, asked Haydn for an opera. The opera, *Orfeo (L'anima del filosofo)*, was not performed, due to intrigues by the rival Pantheon Theatre, the patron of which was the King himself. Although Haydn had received his honorarium in advance and suffered no financial loss, this failure remained the most painful memory of his trip to England.

231 EXCERPT FROM AN
AUTHENTIC COPY OF
THE OPERA 'ORFEO'
('L'ANIMA DEL FILOSOFO')
(HOBOKEN XXVIII: 13)

126

Anna Storace

Mich. Okelly

During his stay in London, Haydn studied English diligently. His first composition written to an English text was the madrigal with orchestral accompaniment, *The Storm*, performed on 24th February, 1792.

235 (LEFT) FELICE
GIARDINI (1716–1796),
COMPOSER AND VIOLINIST

236 (RIGHT) THE SINGER
ELIZABETH BILLINGTON
(C. 1768–1818)

237 THE SINGER GERTRUD
ELISABETH MARA,
B. SCHMELING (1749–1833)

*MADAM-MARA as ARMIDA.*

*During his first eighteen-month stay in London he sought (as we know) to become acquainted with celebrated musicians. Among these was known to him the name of Giardini ... The Lord and Haydn went along ... clearly heard the answer that Giardini gave his servant in a loud voice and that may be literally translated thus: 'I do not want to know that German dog.' (Dies)*

128

238 (LEFT) THE
COMPOSER AND PIANIST
JOHANN LUDWIG
(LADISLAUS) DUSSEK
(1760–1812)

239 (RIGHT) THE VIOLINIST
AND IMPRESARIO
WILHELM CRAMER
(1745–1799)

240 THE COMPOSER AND
PIANIST ADALBERT
GYROWETZ (1763–1850)

*Today, 14th January 1792, the life
of Madam Bilingthon [ Billington ]
was published in print ... It is said
that her character is the worst sort,
but that she is a great genius, and
all the women hate her because she
is so beautiful ... On 1st June 1792
Mara gave her benefit concert. They
played two of my Symphonies, and
I accompanied her, all by myself
at the pianoforte, in a very difficult
English Aria by Purcell. The audience was very small.*
(From Haydn's First London
Notebook)

241 THE ASTRONOMER
WILHELM HERSCHEL
(1738–1822)

*On 15th June I went from Windsor to [Slough] to Doctor Hershel, where I saw the great telescope. It is 40 feet long and 5 feet in diameter. The machinery is very big, but so ingenious that a single man can put it in motion with the greatest ease. There are also 2 smaller of which one is 22 feet long and magnifies 6,000 times. The King had 2 made for himself, each of which measures 12 feet. He paid him 1,000 guineas for them. In his younger days Dr. Hershel was in the Prussian service as an oboe player. During the seven-years' war he deserted with his brother and went to England, where he supported himself as a musician for many years: he became an organist at Bath, but gradually turned more to astronomy . . . Sometimes he sits for 5 or 6 hours under the open sky in the bitterest cold weather.* (From Haydn's First London Notebook)

242 CAMBRIDGE,
KING'S COLLEGE

*...I passed through the little town of Cambridge. Saw the universities there, which are very
conveniently situated, one after another, in a row, but each one separate from the other...*
(From Haydn's Second London Notebook, November, 1791)

131

243 GEORGE, PRINCE
OF WALES (1762–1830)

244 VIEW FROM THE
DUKE OF YORK'S
HOUSE AT OATLANDS

*I must take this opportunity of informing Your Grace that 3 weeks ago I was invited by the Prince of Wales to visit his brother, the Duke of York, at the latter's country seat. The Prince presented me to the Duchess, the daughter of the King of Prussia, who received me very graciously and said many flattering things. She is the most delightful lady in the world, is very intelligent, plays the pianoforte and sings very nicely. I had to stay there 2 days, because a slight indisposition prevented her attending the concert on the first day. On the 2nd day, however, she remained continually at my side from 10 o'clock in the evening, when the music began, to 2 o'clock in the morning. Nothing but Haydn was played. I directed the symphonies from the pianoforte, and the sweet little thing sat beside me on my left and hummed all the pieces from memory, for she had heard them so often in Berlin. The Prince of Wales sat on my right side and played with us on his violoncello, quite tolerably. I had to sing, too. The Prince of Wales is having my portrait painted just now, and the picture is to hang in his room. The Prince of Wales is the most handsome man on God's earth; he has an extraordinary love of music and a lot of feeling, but not much money. Nota bene, this is between ourselves. I am more pleased by his kindness than by any financial gain. On the third day the Duke of York sent me two stages with his own span, since I couldn't catch the mail-coach...* (Haydn to Frau von Genzinger, 20 December, 1791)

*...I never in my life wrote so much in one year as I have here during this past one, but now I am almost completely exhausted, and it will do me good to be able to rest a little when I return home. At present I am working for Salomon's concerts, and I am making every effort to do my best, because our rivals, the Professional Concert, have had my pupil Pleyel from Strassburg come here to conduct their concerts. So now a bloody harmonious war will commence between master and pupil. The newspapers are all full of it, but it seems to me that there will soon be an armistice, because my reputation is so firmly established here. Pleyel behaved so modestly towards me upon his arrival that he won my affection again. We are very often together, and this does him credit, for he knows how to appreciate his father. We shall share our laurels equally and each go home satisfied.* (Haydn to Frau von Genzinger, 17 January, 1792)

*...For some time I was quite beside myself about his [Mozart's] death, and I could not believe that Providence would so soon claim the life of such an indispensable man. I only regret that before his death he could not convince the English, who walk in darkness in this respect, of his greatness—a subject about which I have been sermonizing to them every single day...* (Haydn to Johann Michael Puchberg, January, 1792)

247 HAYDN. PORTRAIT
BY THOMAS HARDY IN
1792, ON THE COMMISSION
OF MUSIC PUBLISHER
JOHN BLAND

248 Haydn. Engraving
by Thomas Hardy from
his own painting

249 THE CORONATION
OF EMPEROR FRANZ II
IN THE CATHEDRAL OF
FRANKFURT ON
14TH JULY, 1792

250 PAUL ANTON II
ESTERHÁZY (1738–1794),
HAYDN'S THIRD PRINCELY
PATRON

*My dear Polzelli!*
*I received your letter with the false news*
*about my wife: in fact she is not quite well,*
*but with her usual sicknesses she may, if*
*she pulls through, outlive me by many years.*
*Well, we shall have to leave her fate to*
*Providence.* I SHALL LEAVE LONDON AT THE
END OF THIS MONTH, *and shall write you*
*from Frankfurt. Yesterday I heard that my*
*Prince will go there as Bohemian Ambassa-*
*dor and will arrive on the 25th of this month,*
*together with his musicians. I think, there-*
*fore, that I shall have to stay with him for*
*a time . . .* (Haydn, 13 June, 1792)

251 BAD GODESBERG,
WHERE HAYDN IS
BELIEVED TO HAVE MET
BEETHOVEN

*Serene Electoral Highness!*
*I humbly take the liberty of sending Your Serene Electoral Highness some musical works,*
*viz., a Quintet, an eight-part Parthie, an oboe Concerto, Variations for the fortepiano, and*
*a Fugue, compositions of my dear pupil Beethoven, with whose care I have been graciously*
*entrusted. I flatter myself that these pieces, which I may recommend as evidence of his*
*assiduity over and above his actual studies, may be graciously accepted by Your Serene*
*Electoral Highness. Connoisseurs and non-connoisseurs alike must candidly admit, from*
*these present pieces, that Beethoven will in time fill the position of one of Europe's greatest*
*composers, and I shall be proud to be able to speak of myself as his teacher; I only wish*
*that he might remain with me a little while longer.* (Haydn to the Elector Maximilian
Franz, 23 November, 1793)

252 (LEFT) LUDWIG VAN
BEETHOVEN (1770–1827),
WHO ARRIVED IN VIENNA
IN NOVEMBER 1792 'TO
RECEIVE MOZART'S SPIRIT
FROM HAYDN'S HANDS'.

253 (RIGHT)
JOSEPH WEIGL (1766–1846),
HAYDN'S FRIEND AND
GODSON

254 A LETTER FROM
PIETRO POLZELLI
(1777–1796), ONE OF
HAYDN'S BEST LOVED
PUPILS, TO HIS MOTHER,
LUIGIA POLZELLI IN
BOLOGNA

255 THE DONOR OF THE MONUMENT, KARL LEONHARD IX, COUNT VON HARRACH (1765–1831), WITH HIS FAMILY

*I considered it fitting and proper, as well as an honour for my park, to erect in the castle precincts surrounding his birthplace a stone monument to the estimable and celebrated J. Haydn . . . I used a part of my garden rather thickly overgrown with various leaf-bearing trees, and a place where the Leitha is quite broad and deep and makes a sudden bend . . . Two sides of the monument are provided with inscriptions . . . the first tablet reads as follows:* TO THE MEMORY / OF JOSEPH HAYDN / THE DEATHLESS MASTER / OF MUSIC, / TO WHOM EAR AND HEART / CONTENDING DO HOMAGE, / DEDICATED, / BY / KARL LEONHARD COUNT VON HARRACH. / IN THE YEAR 1793. *The second tablet bears the short inscription:* ROHRAU / GAVE HIM LIFE / IN THE YEAR 1732 THE 1ST APRIL / EUROPE / UNDIVIDED APPROVAL, / THE 31ST MAY 1809. / THE ENTRANCE TO THE ETERNAL / HARMONIES. (Dies, quoting from a letter by Count von Harrach)

256 THE MONUMENT AS IT LOOKS NOW

257 THE ORIGINAL SURROUNDINGS OF THE MONUMENT

*[On his second journey to England, in 1794] Haydn passed through Passau, where he decided to spend the night. He learned on his arrival that on that very evening his* Seven Words *were going to be performed and that the local Hofkapellmeister had composed accompanying vocal parts for the work. Haydn was satisfied with the performance, but when telling the story added quite simply (and with his usual modesty): '...those vocal parts, I think I would have done them better.'* (Neukomm)

*In Wiesbaden he met with an occurrence which, unimportant in itself, nevertheless gave him pleasure. At the inn where Haydn had stopped, he heard next his room the beloved Andante with the Drum Stroke [Symphony No. 94] being played on a pianoforte. Counting the player a friend, he stepped politely into the room where he heard the music. He found several Prussian officers, all great admirers of his music, who, when he finally made himself known, would not take his word for it that he was Haydn. 'Impossible! Impossible! You Haydn?—Already such an old man!—That doesn't rhyme with the fire in your music!—No! We shall never believe it!'* (Dies)

On the 19th January of 1794, Haydn set out on his journey, accompanied by Elssler. He arrived in London on the 4th of February. During his second stay in England, there was no longer any professional competition for him. During the 1794 season Haydn worked with Salomon's orchestra, and after the dissolution of this orchestra, with the orchestra of the Opera Concerts during the 1795 season. His reputation as well as his financial success was unparalleled.

260 VIEW OF LONDON FROM THE SOUTH

261 THE FAMOUS
DOUBLE-BASS VIRTUOSO
DOMENICO DRAGONETTI
(1763–1846)

262 JOHN FIELD
(1782–1837), 'A YOUNG
BOY, WHICH [SIC] PLAYS THE
PIANO-FORTE EXTREMELY
WELL.' (FROM HAYDN'S
THIRD LONDON NOTEBOOK)

J.B. VIOTTI.

263 THE COMPOSER AND
VIOLINIST GIOVANNI
BATTISTA VIOTTI
(1755–1824)

264 THE COMPOSER AND
PIANIST MUZIO CLEMENTI
(1752–1832)

266 THE DRAMATIC
SOPRANO BRIGITTA BANTI
(1756–1806), FOR WHOM
HAYDN WROTE HIS
'SCENA DI BERENICE'
(HOBOKEN XXIVA: 10,
1795)

The Celebrated
SIGNOR MORELLI.

Birgitta Banti Veneta

267 THE SOPRANO
ANNA MORICHELLI

The Celebrated
MADAM MORICHELLI

On May 4, 1795, I gave my Benefit Concert in the Haymarket Theatre. The hall was filled with a select company. (a) First part of the Military Symphony; Aria
(Rovedino); Concerto (Ferlandy), the first time; Duet
(Morichelli and Morelli) by me; a new symphony in
D, the twelfth and last of the English; (b) second part of
the Military Symphony; Aria (Morichelli); Concerto
(Viotti), Scena nuova by me, Mad. Banti (She song
very scanty) [sic]. The whole company was thoroughly
pleased, and I too. I made this evening four thousand
gulden. One can do this only in England. (Griesinger,
from Haydn's Fourth London Notebook)

145

268 (Left) The composer
William Shield
(1748–1829)

269 (Right) The organist
and conductor of
Handel's works
Joah Bates (1741–1799)

270 Dr. Samuel Arnold
(1740–1802), organist
of Westminster Abbey

271 Dr. William Parsons
(1746–1817), Master of
the King's Band

272 Dr. John Wall
Calcott (1766–1821),
Haydn's pupil

*In the year 1794 Dr. Haydn, Dr. Arnold, Mr. John Stafford Smith, and Mr. Atterbury*
*declared their readiness to cooperate with Dr. Cooke, Dr. Hayes, Dr. Dupuis, Dr. Parsons,*
*Mr. Calcott, the Revd. Osborne Wight, Mr. Webber, Mr. Shield, and Mr. Stevens in their*
*Exertions towards perfecting a work for the Improvement of Parochial Psalmody.*
*as a Small Token of esteem for*
*his abilities and of gratitude*
*for his Services this Piece of*
*Plate is presented to Doctor Haydn*
*by W. D. Tattersall.*
(From Haydn's Third London Notebook)

*On 28th March 1795, I saw the Opera 'Acis & Galathea' by Bianchi. The music is very rich in parts for the wind instruments, and I rather think one would hear the principal melody better if it were not so richly scored.* (From Haydn's Third London Notebook)

275 JOSEPH HAYDN.
DRAWING BY
GEORGE DANCE (20TH
MARCH, 1794, VERSION B)

276 JOHANN PETER
SALOMON. DRAWING BY
GEORGE DANCE

149

277 View of Bath

278 The castrato
Venanzio Rauzzini
(1746–1810)

*On 2nd August 1794, I left at 5 o'clock in the morning for Bath... I lived at the house of Herr Rauzzini, a* Musicus *who is very famous, and who in his time was one of the greatest singers. He has lived there 19 years, supports himself by the Subscription Concerts which are given in the Winter, and by giving lessons... Bath is one of the most beautiful cities in Europe. All the houses are built of stone.. there are a lot of beautiful squares, on which stand the most magnificent houses, but which cannot be reached by any vehicle: they are now building a brand new, broad street.*

*The Castle at Newport has a well 300 feet deep which is driven by a mule. Newport is a nice little town; the people look just like the Germans and mostly have black hair...*

*Mr. Orde is* gouverneur *at Fernhall on the Isle of Wight, whose country house commands the most magnificent view over the ocean.* (From Haydn's Third London Notebook)

150

279 THE COMPOSER
DR. HENRY HARINGTON
(1727–1816), TO WHOM
HAYDN DEDICATED
A SONG
('WHAT ART EXPRESSES',
HOBOKEN XXVIB: 3)

280 FERNHILL, THE
GOVERNOR'S HOUSE,
ISLE OF WIGHT

151

*On 9th July, I left at 5 o'clock in the morning for Portsmouth... I inspected the fortifications there, which are in good repair... I went aboard the French ship-of-the-line called* Le Just; *it has 80 cannons; the English, or rather Lord Howe, captured it... The ship is terribly shot to pieces. The great mast, which is 10 feet 5 inches in circumference, was cut off at the very bottom and lay stretched on the ground. A single cannonball, which passed through the captain's room, killed 14 sailors.* (From Haydn's Third London Notebook)

282 ADMIRAL RICHARD
LORD HOWE (1726–1799)

*Bristol from Rownham Ferry*

*On the 6th I went from Bath 11 miles to Pristol [sic]... The city is very large and half of it, too, is built on a rise. The River flows through the middle of the city, and many hundred merchant ships lie at anchor in the river. There is a great deal of trade... The churches—there are a great many—are all in the old Gothic style...*
*From there to Winschester [sic], where there is a beautiful Gothic Cathedral Church...*
(From Haydn's Third London Notebook)

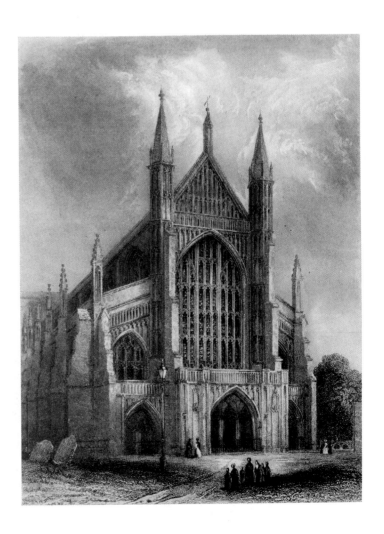

285 THE PALACE AT
HAMPTON COURT

On the way to Portsmuth [sic] I saw the
old Royal Castle at Hampton Court,
which is very large and has a garden like
that at Estoras, with three principal al-
lées; there are various splendid statues
in bronze, and very fine marble vases;
especially beautiful the painting over the
main staircase and the ceiling by the artist
Verrio. This castle is mostly inhabited
by aristocratic widows of the military.
(From Haydn's Third London Notebook)

286 THE PAINTER
PHILIPP JACOB
LOUTHERBOURG
(1740–1812), WHOM
HAYDN MET DURING
HIS SECOND STAY
IN ENGLAND

154

On 1st February 1795, I was invited by the Prince of Wales to attend a musical soirée
at the Duke of York's, which the King, the Queen, her whole family, the Duke of Orange & c.
attended. Nothing else except my own compositions was played; I sat at the pianoforte;
finally I had to sing, too. The King, who hitherto could or would only hear Handel's music,
was attentive; he chatted with me, and introduced me to the Queen, who said many compli-
mentary things to me. (From Haydn's Fourth London Notebook)

The King and the Queen wished to keep him in England. 'You shall have a place in Windsor
in the summers,' said the Queen, 'and then,' she added with an arch look toward the King,
'we shall sometimes make music tête à tête.' 'Oh!' replied the King, 'I am not worked up
over Haydn, he is a good honest German gentleman.' 'To keep that reputation,' answered
Haydn, 'is my greatest pride.' On repeated urging to remain in England, Haydn claimed
that he was bound by gratitude to his Prince's house, and that he could not separate himself
forever from his fatherland or from his wife. (Griesinger)

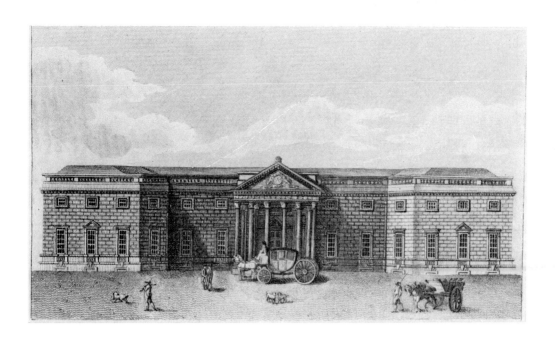

*On 8th Apr. 1795, the marriage took place between the Prince of Wales and the Princess of Brunswick. On the 10th, I was invited to a musical soirée at the Prince of Wales' in Carlton House. An old Symphony was played, which I accompanied on the pianoforte; then a Quartet; and afterwards I had to sing some German and English songs. The Princess sang with me, too; she played a Concerto on the pianoforte quite nicely.* (From Haydn's Fourth London Notebook)

289 PRINCESS CAROLINE
OF BRUNSWICK, THE
WIFE OF THE PRINCE
OF WALES (1768–1821)

*On 3rd Feb., I was invited to the Prince of Wales'; on 15th, 17th and 19th Apr. 1795, I was there again, and on the 21st at the Queen's in Buckingham House.* (From Haydn's Fourth London Notebook)

291 CHARLOTTE, QUEEN
OF ENGLAND (1744–1818)

*I have associated with emperors, kings and many great gentlemen and have heard many
flattering things from them; but I do not wish to live on an intimate footing with such persons,
and I prefer people of my own status.* (Haydn)

FULFILMENT (1795–1809)

293 JOSEPH HAYDN WITH
THE SCORE OF HIS
'SURPRISE' SYMPHONY
(HOBOKEN I: 94).
GOUACHE PAINTING BY
JOHANN ZITTERER

159

294 Plan for the reconstruction of the Palace of Eisenstadt in neo-classic style. (By Charles Moreau)

Under Nikolaus II, the head of the Esterházy family after 1794, Eisenstadt—which was nearer to Vienna—became the Esterházy residence again. Haydn once more directed musical life there, but he had far fewer duties than before 1790. His tasks consisted primarily of composing church music, which after 1802 was directed by the young Vice-Kapellmeister Johann Nepomuk Fuchs. Chamber music was directed by Luigi Tomasini, and the opera performances resumed in 1804 by the talented Johann Nepomuk Hummel.

295 Prince Nikolaus II (1765–1833), the highly educated music-lover, the last Esterházy whom Haydn served

297 STAGE SET FOR
MOZART'S 'MAGIC FLUTE'
(K. 620). DESIGNED BY
CARL MAURER, WHO
WAS IN THE PRINCE'S
SERVICE AT EISENSTADT,
FROM 1802

161

298 'THE SEVEN WORDS',
FIRST PAGE OF THE
SCORE OF THE VOCAL
VERSION (ELSSLER'S COPY
WITH COMPLEMENTARY
VOICES IN HAYDN'S
OWN HAND)

The performance of *The Seven Words* in Passau prompted Haydn to compose a vocal
version of this work himself. In 1795–1796 he rewrote this, which was a favourite
composition of his, written ten years earlier—and this served also as a preliminary
study for his last two oratorios. The text was supplied by Baron van Swieten. (Haydn
first had the parts of the original version copied by Johann Elssler, and then entered
the vocal parts and the parts for the new instruments in his own hand.)

299 'THE SEVEN WORDS',
TITLE-PAGE OF THE
BREITKOPF EDITION, 1801
(HOBOKEN XX: 2)

300 First page of the
score of the 'Missa
in tempore belli' or
'Kettledrum' Mass
written at the time
of preparations for war
(Hoboken XXII: 9, 1796)

The six great masses that he created between 1796 and 1802 were the climax of Haydn's
art in this genre. From this time onwards, he wrote no more symphonies; his symphonic
style, which he continued to deepen and to develop, found its full evolution in these
masses. A number of smaller vocal works, choruses and canons composed at the same
period as the oratorios, also show his renewed interest in vocal music.

301 Haydn's manuscript
list of vocal trios and
quartets

302 Plan for
reconstructing the
altar in the private
chapel at Eisenstadt

163

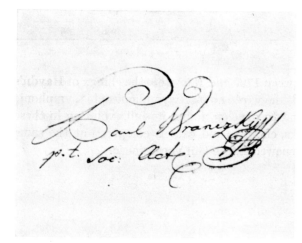

The Tonkünstler-Sozietät ceremonially admitted Haydn as an honorary member in 1797—to correct the injustice committed in 1779. On this occasion Antonio Salieri, with Paul Wranizky, an enthusiastic admirer of Haydn, wrote a letter to the musician who was universally acknowledged as the greatest in Austria.

303 (LEFT) PAUL
WRANIZKY (1756–1808)

304 (RIGHT) EXTRACT
FROM THE MINUTES OF
THE TONKÜNSTLER-
SOZIETÄT

Haydn composed the anthem in 1797, in a general mood of patriotic thought and sentiment, at a time of war and rebellion, to the words of an occasional poem by Lorenz Leopold Haschka. This classically beautiful melody is as simple as a folk song; despite this it is one of Haydn's masterpieces.

306 MANUSCRIPT OF ONE
VERSION OF THE
'GOTT ERHALTE'

165

Pfarr=Kirche St Aegydi

Gumpendorfer = Hauptstrasse.

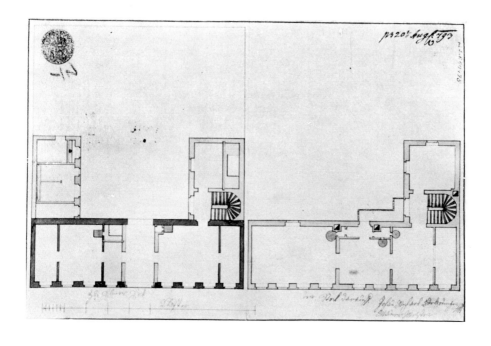

308 Plan for rebuilding
Haydn's house in
Gumpendorf (then a
suburb of Vienna), 1793

166

Abbildung des Haufes in der Vorstadt Windmühle in Wien, in welchem HAYDN den 31. Mai 1809 starb, und in welchem am 1. Juni 1840 die Trauer- u. Erinnrungsfeier Statt fand.

311 SKETCH FOR 'CHAOS'
IN 'THE CREATION'
(HOBOKEN XXI: 2)

312 'THE CREATION'.
FRONTISPIECE FOR THE
VOCAL SCORE OF THE
PLEYEL EDITION

313 FROM THE LIBRETTO,
IN THE HANDWRITING
OF GOTTFRIED VAN
SWIETEN, WITH
INSTRUCTIONS TO THE
COMPOSER ON THE MARGIN

314 BARON GOTTFRIED
VAN SWIETEN (1730–1803)

After having heard the monumental Handel Concerts in London, Haydn began to entertain the idea of writing an oratorio. He wanted to find the music and style to give an entire nation and all listeners a moral and artistic experience. His oratorio *The Creation* (Hoboken XXI: 2), completed in April 1798, was the perfect achievement of his purpose.

The well-known music-lover Gottfried van Swieten wrote a German libretto after the English text by Lidley. Van Swieten roused the composer to anger by giving instructions here and there concerning the character and form the music should take.

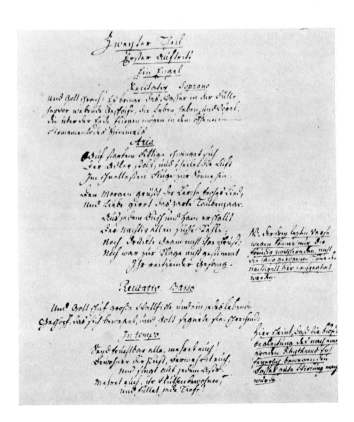

315 (Left) Joseph Haydn.
Porcelain bust
by Anton Grassi
(Version A, 1802;
another version,
plaster cast, made in
1799, without a wig,
is lost)

316 (Right) Joseph
Haydn. Porcelain bust
by Anton Grassi
(Version B)

317 THE SCHWARZENBERG
PALACE ON THE
MEHLMARKT (NOW NEUER
MARKT) IN VIENNA
(BACK CENTRE), WHERE
THE FIRST PERFORMANCE
OF 'THE CREATION'
TOOK PLACE ON THE 29TH
AND 30TH APRIL OF 1798,
BEFORE A SELECT AUDIENCE

*I was there and can assure you I have never experienced anything like it. The flower of Vienna's literary and musical life assembled in the hall . . . Deep silence, tense attention, and I might say—religious devotion prevailed from the moment the violins started. (Carpani)*

318 THE BASS IGNAZ
SAAL, ONE OF THE
SOLOISTS AT THE FIRST
PERFORMANCE

*On the 19th inst. I heard Haydn's* Creation. *Not to report to you this good fortune (for I declare it as such)— would betray either too little feeling for the arts or too little for friendship. The attendance was extraordinary, and receipts amounted to 4088 fl. 30 kr.—a sum never before taken by a Viennese theatre. In addition, the nobility paid all the not inconsiderable costs. It is hard to imagine the silence and attention with which the entire oratorio was received, only softly interrupted by low calls in the most conspicuous places, and received with enthusiastic applause at the end of each piece and section.* (Allgemeine Musikalische Zeitung, *March, 1799*)

321 The Burgtheater
(right) in Vienna,
where the first public
performance of 'The
Creation' took place
on March 19th, 1799

322 Joseph Leopold
Eybler (1765–1846), who
recited the poem by
Gabriela Baumberg
about 'The Creation'

323 The poem by
Gabriela Baumberg
(1775–1839) for the
occasion of the public
performance of
'The Creation'

An den grossen
unsterblichen Hayden.

Erquikend — sanft — wie alles Schöne
Und feurig — wie gerechter Wein,
Ströhmt oft der Zauber *Deiner* Töne
Durch's Ohr, in unser Herz hinein.

Jüngst schuf *Dein* Schöpferisches Werde!
Den Donner, durch den Paukenschall;
Und Himmel — Sonne — Mond — und Erde,
Die Schöpfung ganz — zum Zweitenmal.

Gefühlvoll — staunend — wonnetrunken!
Wie Adam einst im Paradies,
Am Arm der Eva hingesunken
Zwar sprachlos den Erschaffer pries;

So huld'gen wir im Aug die Thräne
Dem Kunstwerk deiner Phantasie —
Der Allmacht deiner Zaubertöne
Und *Dir*, dem Gott der Harmonie!

Von
Gabriela von Baumberg,
bey Gelegenheit als die *Schöpfung*,
diess Meisterstück der Tonkunst, im k. k. Nationaltheater aufgeführt wurde.
Am 19. März 1799.

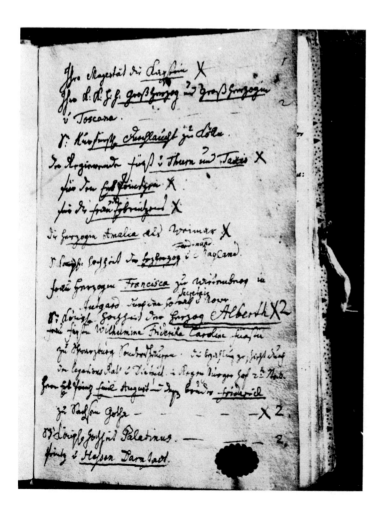

326 PEST-BUDA, THE
CAPITAL OF HUNGARY
AROUND 1800

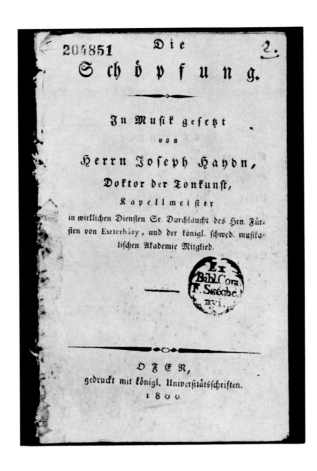

Die
Schöpfung.

In Musik gesetzt
von

Herrn Joseph Haydn,
Doktor der Tonkunst,
Kapellmeister
in wirklichen Diensten Sr. Durchlaucht des Hrn. Fürsten von Eszterházy, und der königl. schwed. musikalischen Akademie Mitglied.

OFEN,
gedruckt mit königl. Universitätsschriften.
1800

327 TEXT OF THE FIRST
PERFORMANCE OF 'THE
CREATION' IN HUNGARY,
CONDUCTED BY HAYDN

One of the first performances abroad of *The Creation* took place in Buda on 8th March, 1800, on the occasion of the festivities organized in honour of the Palatine Josef Anton Johann and his young wife Pawlowna Alexandra. While in Vienna, the Princess (daughter of Tzar Paul I) had asked Haydn to participate. Haydn came to Buda on 16th February in order to direct the performance in person. This was his only visit to the capital of Hungary.

329 TITLE-PAGE OF THE
FIRST EDITION OF THE
'ERDŐDY' QUARTETS
(HOBOKEN III: 75–80)

The Viennese classical style achieved in the
six string quartets Opus 76 (1797) a final
concentration, a last condensation before its
dissolution into Romanticism. The total impression of the music is still classical, but several particulars—especially the romantic
deviations in harmony, the loose freeing of
the ostinato rhythm, and the veiled melancholy of some melodies—anticipate later
achievements by Beethoven and Schubert.

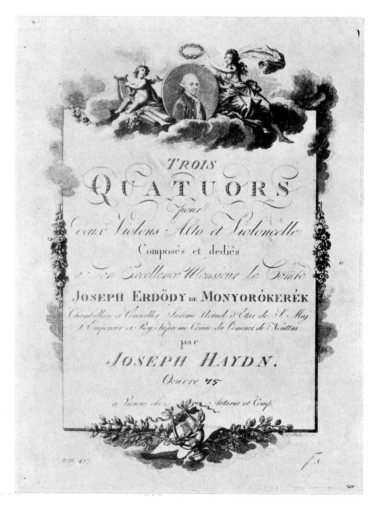

330 From the manuscript
of the Quartet in
F major, Opus 77
(Hoboken III: 82)

331 Josef Franz Max,
Prince Lobkowitz
(1772–1816), to whom
Haydn dedicated his
String Quartets
Opus 77
(Hoboken III: 81–82)
and later, Beethoven
his first Quartets,
Opus 18

*L'istesso tuono* (E flat = D sharp), Haydn instructed the performer on his unusual modulation of the E-flat minor and E-minor keys placed next to each other in the first movement of his F-major Quartet Opus 77.

177

The visit by Admiral Nelson and Lady Hamilton in September 1800 was a great event at the Prince's residence in Eisenstadt. In honour of the Admiral, Haydn's *Missa in angustiis*, later called the *Nelson Mass*, was performed (Hoboken XXII: 11). Lady Hamilton sang, accompanied by Haydn on the piano, the Cantata *Arianna a Naxos* (Hoboken XXVIB: 2).

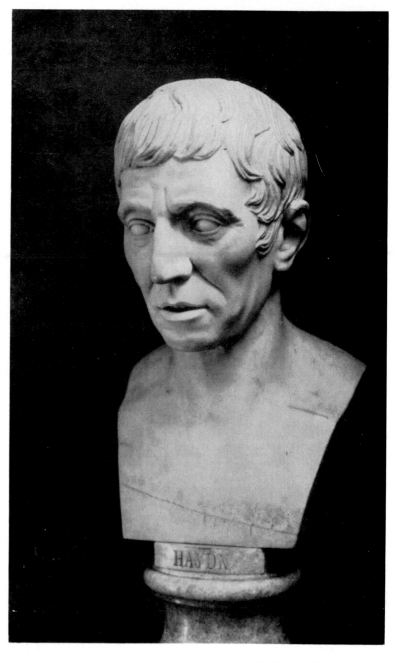

332 JOSEPH HAYDN. MARBLE BUST 'BY AUGUST ROBATZ MADE FROM NATURE' (*c.* 1800)

333 FROM THE MANUSCRIPT OF 'LINES FROM THE BATTLE OF THE NILE', WHICH HAYDN WROTE IN 1798 FOR THE GLORIFICATION OF NELSON'S VICTORY (HOBOKEN XXVIb: 4)

334 ADMIRAL LORD
NELSON (1758–1805)

335 LADY HAMILTON
(1761–1815)

336 A BROADWOOD
HARPSICHORD FROM
HAYDN'S ESTATE

179

337 Joseph Haydn.
Unsigned lead bust
(*c.* 1800?), bequeathed
in Haydn's will to
the Harrach family

338 Joseph Haydn.
Unsigned wax bust
(c. 1800?), believed to
be by Franz Christian
Thaller (Version B)

181

Van Swieten, whose enthusiasm was fired by the success of *The Creation*, surprised Haydn with a new libretto, *The Seasons* (Hoboken XXI: 3), a re-writing of James Thomson's didactic poem. Haydn worked on the oratorio from 1799 to 1801. The primitive style demanded by van Swieten frequently annoyed Haydn before he succeeded in creating a form which he did not consider unworthy of his art.

339 EMPRESS MARIA THERESA, WHO SANG THE SOPRANO SOLO IN BOTH OF HAYDN'S ORATORIOS AT COURT PERFORMANCES

340 'THE SEASONS', NEUKOMM'S PIANO SCORE FROM 'AUTUMN'

341 The Redoutensaal (on the right), where the first public performance of 'The Seasons' took place on the 29th May 1801. (In the centre and on the left, the Court Library, which was in van Swieten's charge)

DIE JAHRESZEITEN
nach Thomson
in Musik gesetzt von
JOSEPH HAYDN
PARTITUR

Originalausgabe.

342 Title-page of the first edition of 'The Seasons', 1802

183

*The French artists, gathered together in the* Théâtre des arts *to perform that immortal
work, the* Creation of the World, *composed by the celebrated* HAYDN, *are filled with a just
admiration for his genius, and beg him to accept the homage of their respect, of the enthusiasm which inspired them, and the medal which they have struck in his honour.*
*No year goes by in which a new product of this composer does not enchant the artists,
enlighten their minds, contribute to the progress of the art, widen the immense spaces of
harmony, and prove that its expanses are boundless if one follows the luminous torch with
which* HAYDN *has brilliantly illuminated the present and which points the way to the
future. But the imposing conception of the* ORATORIO *even surpasses, if such a thing be
possible, everything which this wise composer has hitherto offered to an astonished Europe.
When in this work* HAYDN *imitates the* FIRE OF HEAVEN, *he seems to have portrayed
himself, and thus persuades us all that his name will shine fully as long as the stars whose
rays he seems to have absorbed.*
*P. S. If we here admire the skill and the talent by means of which Citizen* GATTEAUX
*has so well reflected our intentions in the engraving of the medal we offer to* HAYDN, *we
must also pay tribute to the loftiness of his sentiments, for he has been content to receive for
his efforts merely the glory which is his today.* (To Haydn from 142 French musicians,
20 July,1801)

*Gentlemen,*
*It is the privilege of especially great artists to confer renown, and who can have greater claims to such a noble prerogative than you? You, who combine the most thorough and profound theory with the most skilful and perfect execution, who cast a veil over the composer's deficiencies, and who often discover therein beauties which the composer himself did not suspect. By thus embellishing* The Creation *you have earned the right to share in the approbation with which this composition was received. The public, too, echoes the just tribute which I must pay to you here: their appreciation of your talents is so great that your approbation ensures their own; and thus your approbation in some measure indicates to those on whom it is conferred the anticipated fame of posterity. I have often doubted whether my name would survive me; but your kindness inspires me with confidence, and the token of esteem with which you have honoured me justifies my hope that perhaps* I SHALL NOT WHOLLY DIE. *Yes, gentlemen, you have crowned my grey hairs, and strewed flowers on the brink of my grave. My heart cannot express all that it feels, and I cannot write to you my profound gratitude and devotion. You will know how to appreciate them, however: you, gentlemen, who cultivate the arts from enthusiasm and not for gain, and who regard the gifts of fortune as naught, but fame as everything.* (Haydn's answer, 10 August, 1801)

345 JOSEPH HAYDN.
ENGRAVING BY L. DARCIS
FROM THE DRAWING BY
P. N. GUÉRIN,
ILLUSTRATING THE
'COLLECTION COMPLETTE
DES QUATUORS d'HAYDN',
PUBLISHED BY HAYDN'S
FORMER PUPIL, PLEYEL
IN PARIS

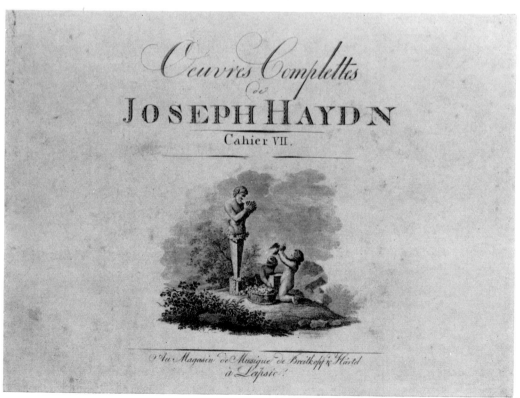

346 TITLE-PAGE OF A
VOLUME OF THE
'OEUVRES COMPLETTES
DE JOSEPH HAYDN',
PUBLISHED IN LEIPZIG
BY BREITKOPF &
HÄRTEL, THROUGH THE
INTERCESSION OF
GEORG AUGUST
GRIESINGER
(CAHIER VII, HOBOKEN
XV: 18–20, 11–13)

347 George Thomson
(1757–1851),
the publisher of
Scottish folk songs

348 An album of
Scottish folk songs
adapted by Haydn
(Hoboken XXXI:
101–150).
published by Napier
in London

*Most esteemed Sir!*
*At last I send you all the remaining Scottish*
*Songs, the composition of which has cost me*
*great effort, for I have been very ill for some*
*time now; but nevertheless I hope that all of*
*them will give at least some pleasure, though*
*it's difficult for a man of seventy-three to be*
*able to satisfy the world. Well, be that as it may,*
*I have done my very best not to disappoint my*
*dear friend . . .* (Haydn to Thomson, 10 May,
1804)

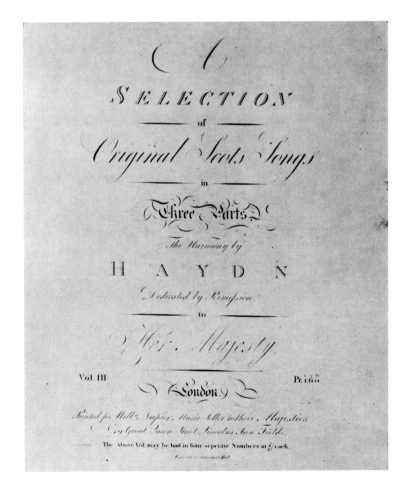

187

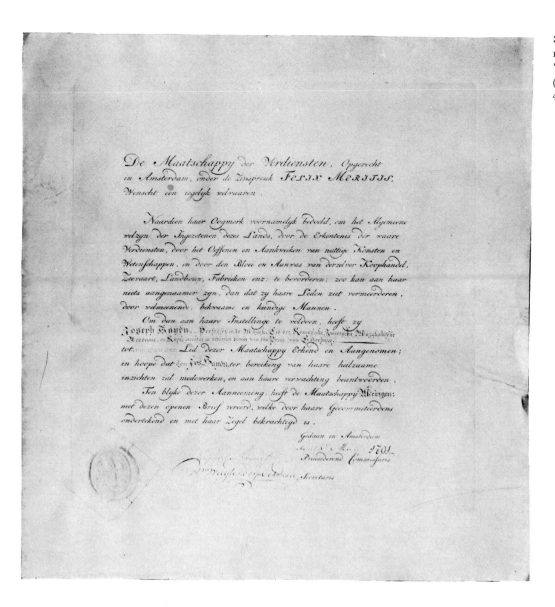

350 JOSEPH HAYDN.
WAX MEDALLION BY
SEBASTIAN IRRWOCH
(1803)

351 FREDERIK SAMUEL
SILVERSTOLPE (1769–1851),
SWEDISH DIPLOMAT IN
VIENNA. HAYDN OWED
TO HIM HIS MEMBERSHIP
OF THE MUSICAL
ACADEMY OF STOCKHOLM
(1798) AND A SWEDISH
TRANSLATION OF 'THE
CREATION' (1801)

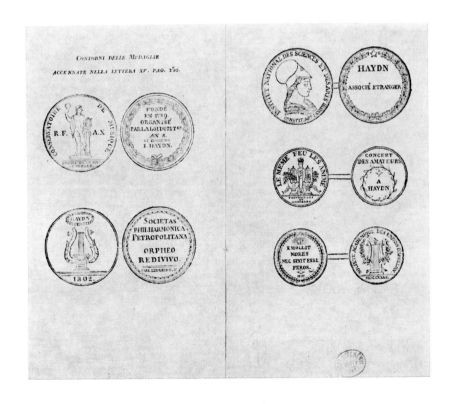

352 COMMEMORATIVE
HAYDN MEDALS
(REPRODUCED IN THE
HAYDN MONOGRAPH BY
GIUSEPPE CARPANI, 1812)

The Philharmonic Society of St. Petersburg was founded in 1802 on the occasion of a performance of Haydn's *Creation*. This explains the date on the medal, which was sent to the maestro in 1808 together with a ceremonial letter. The stimulus to perform Haydn's works in St. Petersburg came from Sigismund Neukomm, whose instrumentation of the oratorio *Il ritorno di Tobia* was approved by Haydn.

*My dear Papa!*              *St. Petersburg, 3/17 April 1807.*

*Yesterday I gave a concert here, the affiche of which I enclose. Your excellent choruses from* Tobia *were received with the great enthusiasm which I have always noticed, with deep satisfaction, is accorded to your unrivalled masterpieces whenever they are performed here. As No. 2 I chose the chorus, 'Ah gran Dio! sol tu sei &c.,' as No. 4 'Odi le nostri voci &c.' and as No. 6, 'Svanisce in un momento' where, even at the end of the first part, they began to applaud with the utmost vigour. I conducted, and the excellent Court Chorus, combined with a selected band of large size, played with such affection that you certainly would have been completely satisfied with the performance, should we have had the good fortune to have had you with us... I am writing you all this because I cannot show you my gratitude in any other way than to assure you that every stroke of good luck which will ever happen to me is only YOUR doing. —You are my father and the creator of my luck.*

*How I envy Vienna for having the good fortune to have you within its walls! How often, dear Papa, I long to see you, even for an hour! Shouldn't this bliss soon be mine?...* (Neukomm)

356 Lines of homage
of a canon dedicated
to Joseph Haydn by
his old friend
Johann Georg
Albrechtsberger

Gior. Michele Haydn

358 Johann Michael
Haydn (1737–1806),
Joseph Haydn's younger
brother

359–361 Pay-roll of
the chamber and choir
musicians of Prince
Esterházy, 1801

In the Summer of 1801 the three Haydn brothers—
Joseph, Michael, then celebrated and famous in Vienna,
and Johann, youngest and least talented, who was a
tenor—met for the last time at Eisenstadt. The list of
Eisenstadt musicians included Johann, with a modest
salary.

362 The signature of
Johann Evangelist
Haydn (1743–1805)

192

363 JOSEPH HAYDN (?)
UNSIGNED PASTEL FROM
THE ESTERHÁZY
COLLECTION

364 TEXT OF THE FOUR-
PART SONG
'THE OLD MAN'
(HOBOKEN XXVC: 5)
IN HAYDN'S
HANDWRITING

365 HAYDN'S MUSICAL
VISITING CARD, WITH HIS
OWN MELODY. ('GONE IS
ALL OF MY OWN
STRENGTH, OLD AND
WEAK AM I')

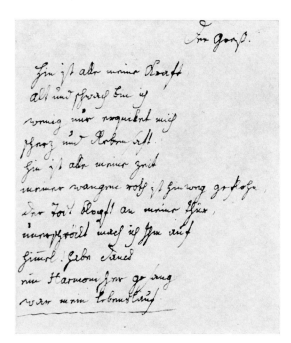

In 1803 Haydn's strength was sufficient only for a frag-
mentary composition. Of his last string quartet—Opus
103 (Hoboken III: 83)—only the slow movement and a
minuet, characterized by a tragic resignation, were
completed. The last page of the first edition (Breitkopf
& Härtel, 1806) ended with his musical visiting card.

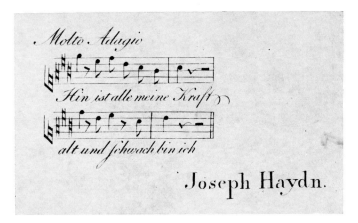

193

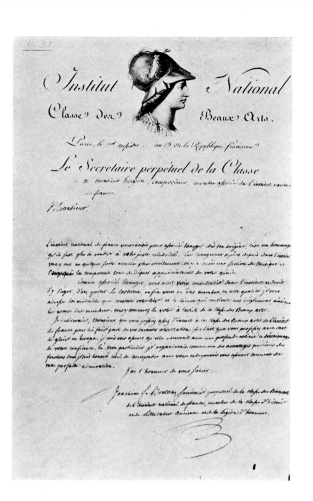

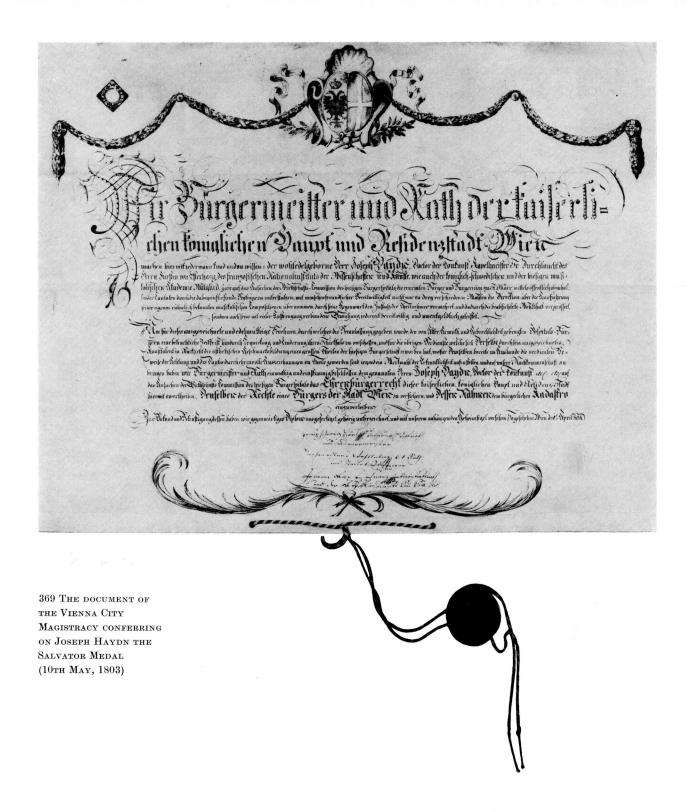

369 The document of
the Vienna City
Magistracy conferring
on Joseph Haydn the
Salvator Medal
(10th May, 1803)

CHERUBINI

The English newspaper *Gentle-men's Magazine* reported Haydn's death in January 1805. Cherubini, who was living in Paris, loved Haydn with the reverence of a son and respected him as a pupil; he was deeply moved by the news and composed his funeral music.

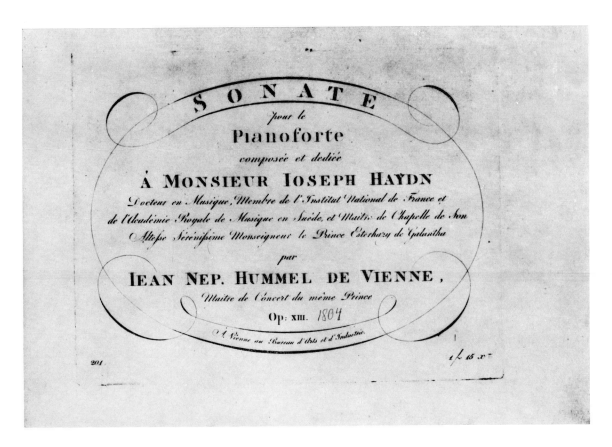

*Dearest Hummel,*
*I terribly regret that I cannot have the pleasure of conducting my little work for the last*
*time, but on the other hand I am convinced that everyone (WITHOUT EXCEPTION) will do*
*everything in their power to support their old Papa, especially since the worthy Hummel*
*will be their guide . . .*
*P. S. My compliments to everyone.*
(Haydn, 28th September, 1804)

*Eisenstadt, 8th October 1804.*
*Most beloved Papa!*
*Since, like an obedient son,*
*I count on the kindly indul-*
*gence of the great musical*
*father, I have dared to dedi-*
*cate the enclosed little piece*
*to you. I was not moved to*
*do so by any desire to shine;*
*but rather the strong feeling*
*of gratitude, of respect and of*
*sincere love which I bear for*
*you—these were the moving*
*factors. If you continue to*
*honour me with your kindly*
*trust and benevolence, then I*
*shall feel entirely happy as*
*    Your devoted son,*
*    Joh. Nep. Hummel, m.p.*

Of Haydn's three authentic biographers, the diplomat Georg August Griesinger had known him the longest. They began to exchange letters in 1799. Griesinger was an honest man, who wrote down his memories of Haydn and kept himself in the background.

The landscape-painter Albert Christoph Dies, who used to visit the aged maestro from 1805 onwards, described the actions and sayings of Haydn in highly colourful language, and added his own impressions.

The poet Giuseppe Carpani met the great composer only in 1808. But since he was an artist himself, we are obliged to him for some valuable informative notes about the working methods and music of Haydn.

374 THE PALACE GARDENS IN EISENSTADT. OIL PAINTING BY ALBERT CHRISTOPH DIES IN THE YEAR HAYDN DIED

375 GIUSEPPE CARPANI (1752–1825)

376 THE PALACE AT
EISENSTADT

*My dear Son!*                                                        *Vienna, 20th March 1808.*

*Your truly heart-warming remarks and those of all the members of the Prince Esterházy
band on the occasion of my name-day, moved me to tears. I thank you and all the others
from the bottom of my heart, and ask you to tell all the members in my name that I regard
them all as my dear children, and beg them to have patience and forbearance with their old,
weak father; tell them that I am attached to them with a truly fatherly love, and that there
is nothing I wish more than to have just sufficient strength so that I could enjoy once more
the harmony of being at the side of these worthy men, who made the fulfilment of my duties
so pleasant. Tell them that my heart will never forget them, and that it is the greatest honour
for me, through the grace of my* ILLUSTRIOUS PRINCE, *to be placed at the head not only
of great artists, but of* NOBLE AND
THANKFUL HUMAN BEINGS. (Haydn
to Antonio Polzelli)

377 ANTONIO POLZELLI
(1783–1855)

378 THE MARIAHILFER
CHURCH NEAR
HAYDN'S HOUSE

*In the name of the Holy Trinity,
God the Father, Son and Holy
Ghost. Amen . . .*
*30. I bequeath to Philipp Schim-
pel, Chormeister in Haimburg,
and to his wife jointly 100 Gulden, as well as . . . the portrait of
her father, named Frank, who
was my first teacher of music . . .*
*33. I bequeath to Madame Aloi-
sia Polzelli, formerly a singer at
His Serene Highness Prince Esterházy's establishment a lifelong
annuity of 150 Gulden . . . but
after her death I bequeath*
*34. that one half of these 150
Gulden, viz. 75 Gulden be given
forever to the two poorest or-
phans in the village of my birth,
Rohrau . . . And the other half,
75 Gulden shall be*
*35. left to the squire of Rohrau
in order to maintain in good
order . . . the monument erected
to me . . .*
*36. I bequeath to my faithful and
honest servant Johann Elssler
6000 Gulden . . .*

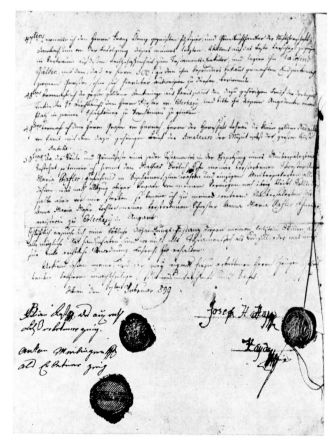

379 FROM THE LAST
WILL AND TESTAMENT OF
HAYDN, DATED 7TH
FEBRUARY, 1809

380 EXTRACT FROM THE
SCORE OF HAYDN'S WORKS,
WHICH WAS COMPILED BY
HIS COPYIST AND
SECRETARY JOHANN
ELSSLER, IN 1805

381 JOSEPH HAYDN.
OIL PAINTING BY
ISIDOR NEUGASS
(1805–6)

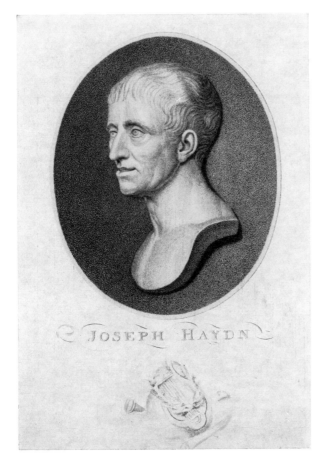

382 JOSEPH HAYDN.
ENGRAVING BY
DAVID WEISS
(ARTARIA EDITION, 1808)

48. I bequeath the large golden commemorative medal from Paris, together with the letter of the Paris musicians pertaining to it, to His Serene Highness Prince Esterházy...

49. I bequeath to Count von Harrach, squire of Rohrau, the little gold medal from Paris with the letter of the Music-Lovers pertaining to it, and the large antique bust.

50. ...I appoint herewith Matthias Fröhlich, son of my deceased sister Anna Maria Rafler, blacksmith of Fischamend, as the true and sole universal heir of everything that is left of my property after deduction of the above legacies. Should this heir die before me, then I appoint as my further universal heiress Anna Maria Moser, daughter of my deceased sister... dressmaker in Eszterháza in Hungary...

Vienna, the 7th February 1809.
Joseph Haydn m.p.

384 THE CEREMONIAL
PERFORMANCE OF 'THE
CREATION'. WATERCOLOUR
BY BALTHASAR WIGAND.
THE SEATED FIGURE IN
THE FOREGROUND IS
JOSEPH HAYDN. (IN THE
RELATIVELY SMALL
ENSEMBLE THE SOPRANO
AND CONTRALTO PARTS
WERE SUNG BY THE
BOYS' CHOIR.)

Haydn appeared in public for the last time on 27th March 1808, when *The Creation* was performed in the Assembly Hall of the Old University. Beethoven, Salieri, Gyrowetz, Hummel and other great Viennese musicians received the aged maestro. Salieri conducted; a festive atmosphere prevailed.

385 MARIA JOSEPHA
HERMENEGILD, PRINCESS
LIECHTENSTEIN
(1768–1845), WIFE OF
NIKOLAUS II, PRINCE
ESTERHÁZY, WHO
COMMISSIONED THE
COMMEMORATIVE CASKET
AND PRESENTED IT TO
HAYDN

386 THE COMMEMORATIVE
CASKET WITH WIGAND'S
WATERCOLOUR ON THE LID

387 Napoleon marching
into Schönbrunn,
10th May, 1809

388 August Wilhelm
Iffland (1759–1814),
the famous actor, who
visited Haydn in
September, 1808

389 THE BOMBARDMENT
OF VIENNA AT NIGHT,
BEFORE THE FRENCH
TROOPS OCCUPIED THE
CITY ON 11TH MAY, 1809

390 JOHANN ELSSLER
(1769–1843), FATHER OF
THE FAMOUS BALLERINA,
FANNY ELSSLER, THE
LAST MEMBER OF THE
ELSSLER FAMILY OF
COPYISTS, WHO WAS THE
MAESTRO'S SECRETARY
AND FAITHFUL SERVANT
DURING THE EVENING OF
HIS LIFE

Haydn's last joy was a visit
by a French officer who
called on him on 26th May,
and sang Haydn an aria from
*The Creation*, accompanying
himself on the piano. That
day Haydn played the *Gott
erhalte* three times on the
piano. Next day, he no longer had the strength to get
up. He passed away on the
31st May, shortly after mid-
night.

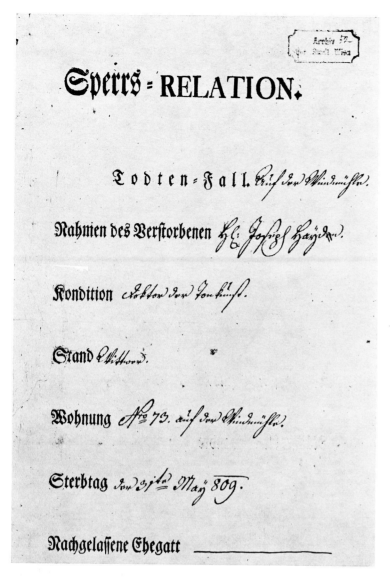

NAME OF THE DECEASED *Joseph Haydn*

PROFESSION *Doctor of Music*

STATUS *Widower*

ADDRESS *No. 73 auf der Windmühle*

DATE OF DEATH *31st May 1809*

SURVIVING SPOUSE − − − − − −

During the troubled times of the occupation of the city, Haydn was buried modestly in the Hundsturm cemetery. However, the musical world paid its final tribute to him in the presence of a great crowd of music-lovers, on 15th June, at more fitting obsequies in the Schottenkirche, at which Mozart's Requiem was performed.

392 THE INVITATION TO
THE MEMORIAL SERVICE

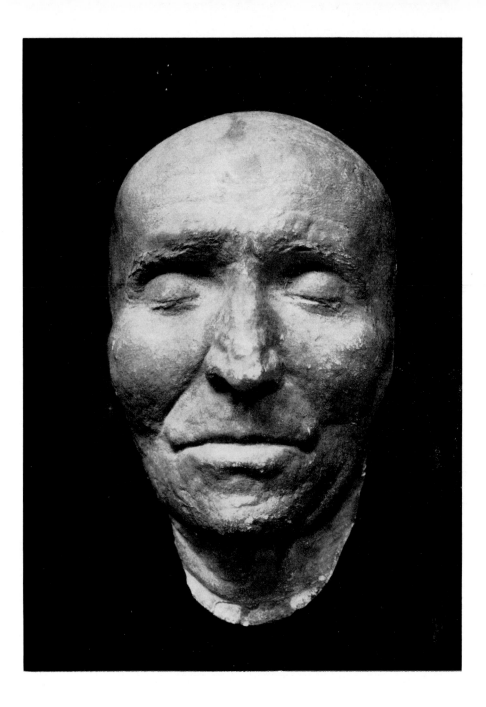

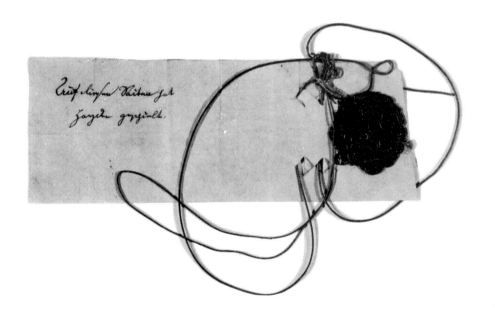

394 'Auf diesen Saiten
hat Haydn gespielt'
[Haydn played on
these strings]. A relic
of Haydn in the
Esterházy Archives

COMMENTARY

ABBREVIATIONS
ICONOGRAPHY OF AUTHENTIC HAYDN PICTURES
LIST OF SOURCES AND ANNOTATIONS

# ABBREVIATIONS

A. M. = *Acta Musicalia*, Documents, files, receipts, etc. from the former Esterházy Archives, now in the Department for Theatrical History of the National Széchényi Library, Budapest.

AmZ = *Allgemeine Musikalische Zeitung*, Leipzig.

Artaria–Botstiber = F. Artaria–H. Botstiber: *Joseph Haydn und das Verlagshaus Artaria*. Vienna, 1909.

Bartha–Somfai = D. Bartha–L. Somfai: *Haydn als Opernkapellmeister*. Budapest–Mainz, 1960.

Botstiber = The chapter 'Haydn-Bildnisse' in the book by Pohl–Botstiber.

Budapest, Nat. Lib. = Országos Széchényi Könyvtár (National Széchényi Library), Budapest, Book Department and its sections: Cartographic Collection, Music Department, Department for Theatrical History.

Budapest, Nat. Mus. = Magyar Nemzeti Múzeum (Hungarian National Museum), Budapest, Collection of Historical Portraits and Collection of Musical Instruments.

Budapest, State Archives = Országos Levéltár, Budapest.

CCLN = *The Collected Correspondence and London Notebooks of Joseph Haydn*, by H. C. Robbins Landon, London, 1959.

Dies = A. Chr. Dies: *Biographische Nachrichten von Joseph Haydn*. Vienna, 1810. (Quoted in German from the new edition by Horst Seeger, Berlin–Kassel, 1959; in English from *Joseph Haydn, Eighteenth-Century Gentleman and Genius*, a translation with introduction and notes by Vernon Gotwals, Madison, 1963.)

Est. Arch., Est. Coll. = Esterházy Archives and Collection; at present divided: 1) Eisenstadt, Palace 2) Budapest, National Széchényi Library (Music Department, Department for Theatrical History), State Archives.

GBA = *Joseph Haydn. Gesammelte Briefe und Aufzeichnungen. Unter Benützung der Quellensammlung von H. C. Robbins Landon herausgegeben und erläutert von Dénes Bartha*. (The collected correspondence and London Notebooks in original language.) Budapest–Kassel, 1965.

Geiringer I = K. Geiringer: *Joseph Haydn*. Potsdam, 1932. (Die grossen Meister der Musik.)

Geiringer II = K. Geiringer: *Joseph Haydn*. Mainz, 1959.

Griesinger = G. A. Griesinger: *Biographische Notizen über Joseph Haydn*. Leipzig, 1910. (Quoted in German from the new edition by Franz Grasberger, Vienna, 1954; in English from *Joseph Haydn, Eighteenth-Century Gentleman and Genius*, a translation with introduction and notes by Vernon Gotwals, Madison, 1963.)

Hoboken = A. van Hoboken: *Joseph Haydn. Thematisch-bibliographisches Werkverzeichnis*. Vol. I: Mainz, 1957. Vol II: in preparation.

Horányi = M. Horányi: *The Magnificence of Eszterháza*. London, 1962.

Landon SofJH = H. C. R. Landon: *The Symphonies of Joseph Haydn*. London, 1959. *Supplement to —*. London, 1961.

Larsen 3HK = J. P. Larsen: *Drei Haydn-Kataloge in Faksimile*. Copenhagen, 1941.

Muller = J. Muller: 'Haydn Portraits.' *The Musical Quarterly* XVIII, No. 2. 1932. Haydn-Number.

Pohl I, II = C. F. Pohl: *Joseph Haydn*. Vol. I: 1875 (1878), Vol. II: 1882.

Pohl–Botstiber = Volume III of the book *Joseph Haydn* by C. F. Pohl. Leipzig, 1927.

Schnerich = A. Schnerich: *Joseph Haydn und seine Sendung*. Second edition. Vienna, 1926.

Vienna, GdMF = Bibliothek der Gesellschaft der Musikfreunde, Vienna.

Vienna, Mus. d. Stadt = Historisches Museum der Stadt Wien.

Vienna, ÖNB = if no other reference, Portrait Collection and Pictorial Archives of the Österreichische Nationalbibliothek, Vienna.—Also other sections: Cartographic Collection, PhA ('Archiv für Photogramme musikalischer Meisterhandschriften...').

Vogel = E. Vogel: 'Joseph Haydn-Portraits.' *Jahrbuch der Musikbibliothek Peters für 1898*.

The following attempt at an iconography is limited to portraits of Haydn that have been verified as authentic by the author with certainty or at least a high degree of probability. Those pictures have been considered of which the originals have survived or of which contemporary copies and photographs represent lost original pictures. Only those pictures count as authentic or historic to the author which can be guaranteed by contemporary written documents. The criterion for judging the rest of the pictures has been the careful investigation of their production and comparison with undoubtedly authentic pictures.

Yet the history of production and lifelike artistic reproduction are different factors in the judging of authenticity. For instance, there is no doubt as to the authenticity of pictures Nos. **2** and **20**, in spite of their lack of similarity with other portraits, because of the documented history of their production; while the true and convincing reproduction of Haydn's characteristic features speak for the authenticity of pictures Nos. **3, 5,** and **6**, the origin of which is unclear. The introductory chapter has a comparative examination of those features in the portraits which, in the author's view, are among the most important ones. The different focus and artistic conception allow a fairly exact reconstruction of the living model. (See pictures Nos. **3, 8, 9, 10, 11, 12, 15, 16, 17, 18, 19, 23** on pages XIV–XV.) Pictures Nos. **4, 5,** and **6** are important on account of the characteristic profile. Nos. **2, 7,** and **13** seem to be somewhat idealized; No. **20** bears witness to the lack of skill of the young artist; on the small full portrait of No. **22**, Haydn's features are practically unrecognizable. Because it has little similarity with later authentic pictures No. **1** is a special case; one should remember, however, that the true picture of Haydn which is closest in time (No. **3**) was produced at least fifteen years later.

We believe we have established sufficiently in the Supplement the reasons for the listing of pictures Nos. **24** to **26**. Finally we ought to mention some of the engravings after authentic paintings and pieces of sculpture (especially Nos. **2, 10, 12, 14, 15**) which originated during Haydn's lifetime and which have not been included in this iconography nor amongst the illustrations of this book. The analytical-comparative material in the Picture Appendix (**a–i**, pages 224–225) is an exception. The rest have been disregarded either because they are only primitive reproductions of the original (or often only of a copy of the latter), or else, the artist, who himself did not know Haydn personally, reproduced the features of the composer wrongly or distorted them.

In view of all these considerations, our list contains far fewer Haydn pictures than the iconographies by Vogel, Marcel, Schnerich, Botstiber and Muller, or the material published in smaller contributions. It is possible that their number will be further reduced in future selections through the application of still more severe criteria, while their number could be increased only through the discovery of hitherto unknown authentic pictures.

The list of pictures is followed with annotated documentary references to the origin of the authentic portraits. The first part (texts **A-I**) contains relevant quotations from Haydn's letters and notebooks. We have had to refrain from quoting some of these references, as for instance from his letter of 10th May 1804 to Thomson, because it is uncertain which engraving Haydn meant. Another example is Haydn's letter of 25th February 1804 to Zelter, in the postscript to which he thanked him for sending the clumsy engraving by Champonnier-Laurens after Hardy (No. **10b**), on which his birth date was given wrongly (as 1733). The second part of the documentary references (texts **K** to **M**) contains quotations from the biographies by Griesinger and Dies, the third part (texts **N** to **Y**) cuttings from Pohl I and Pohl—Botstiber respectively, which cannot be disregarded, since Pohl had at his disposal many almost unknown (or later lost) documents. We hope that such gaps as still remain in the documentary references and in the list of pictures will be filled by future research.

**1** About 1768? Unsigned (GRUNDMANN, Johann Basilius?). Oil painting, 21″×14″.
According to tradition, Prince Nikolaus Esterházy commissioned it for his Eszterháza palace where the picture was probably destroyed in 1945. (Photo by Forstner, Eisenstadt.) *Cf.* text **W**, further annotations to texts **ABCD**.

**2** 1781. MANSFELD, Johann Ernst. Copper engraving (published by Artaria & Co., Vienna), 6″×3½″.
Commissioned by the Artaria Publishing House, engraved in Vienna not later than 1781 from a (lost?) painting sent by Haydn from Eszterháza to Vienna. Mentioned in Haydn's letters. *Cf.* texts **ABCD**.

**3** 1785. SEEHAS, Christian Ludwig. Oil painting, 24″×20½″.
Presumably the painting was commissioned by the Duke of Schwerin, who had sent Seehas to Vienna with a scholarship. ⟨→Ludwigslust, the ducal concert hall; →Schwerin, State Museum.⟩

**4** 1785. LÖSCHENKOHL, Hieronymus. Engraved silhouette (published in the Öst. Nat.-Kalender 1786, Vienna, Chapter 'Geist und Harmonie'), 3½″×2″.
The calendar was announced on the 24th December 1785. The sketch was made presumably in Vienna, not later than February 1785.

**5** *c.* 1788? Anonymous miniature, watercolour on ivory, in a metal frame, 2″ in diameter.
Circumstance of origin unknown. *Cf.* text **X** ⟨→Haydn; Frau J. G. v. Erggelet; →? →Vienna, GdMF.⟩

**6** About 1788? Silhouette by anonymous artist, with frame drawn in ink, 4½″×3½″.
Origin unknown. A later inscription reads: *Joseph Haydn. | Dieser Schattenriss, ein Geschenk des Hrn W. Schulze in Berlin\* | kam aus Haydn's Händen zunächst in Besitz seines Copisten Joh. Elssler. | \*1871* [Joseph Haydn. | This silhouette, a present from Mr. W. Schulze of Berlin\* | was transferred from Haydn's hands first into the possession of his copyist Joh. Elssler. | \*1871.] *Cf.* notes to text **K**. ⟨→Vienna, GdMF.⟩

**\*7** 1791. OTT, A. M. (Bust, Miniature?) lost; see **7a**. Mentioned in Haydn's First and Second London Notebooks. *Cf.* texts **EF, N**.
**7a** 1791. BARTOLOZZI, Francesco, after **\*7** 'A. M. Ott pinx. Painter to the Duke of Orleans.' Engraving (published 4th April 1791 by Humphrey, London), 6½″ in diameter. *Cf.* text **N**.

**8a, 8b** 1791? (GUTTENBRUNN, Ludwig.) Oil painting on wood, in two versions; **a:** First version (or copy of No. **8b**?), 7″×10″; **b:** more elaborate version (model of the engraving by Schiavonetti), 8″×10″.
For unknown client; mentioned in Haydn's First and Second Notebooks. *Cf.* texts **EF**, there the possible origin about 1770. One of the two versions was in the possession of

Haydn's wife and after her death in the composer's own; Kininger made his engraving from it (No. **14**). Scholarship so far has passed over the difference between the two versions, although it is beyond doubt. The **a** version (most probably unsigned and certainly undated) is less elaborate ⟨?; →Prof. Karajan, Graz; →(lost?), Photograph (1898): Museum der Stadt Leipzig, earlier Peters-Bibl.⟩; the **b** version (unsigned, undated) has more details and served as a model for the engraving by L. Schiavonetti from 1792, see picture Appendix **a** ⟨?; → Stefan Zweig; → Mrs. Eva Alberman, London⟩.

**9** 1791. HOPPNER, John. Oil painting, 56″×45″. Commissioned by the Prince of Wales, and painted in London in December 1791. Mentioned in the Second London Notebook and in Haydn's letter of 20th December, 1791. *Cf.* texts **FG.** ⟨→ London, Buckingham Palace; → London, Windsor Castle.⟩

**10a, 10b** 1792. HARDY, Thomas. **a:** Oil painting 30″×25″; **b:** engraving made from this painting (published in 1792 by Bland, London), 8½″×7″. Painted and engraved to the order of the London music publisher John Bland. Mentioned in Haydn's Second London Notebook. *Cf.* text **F.** ⟨**a:** J. Bland; → ? → London, Royal College of Music.⟩

**11a, 11b** 1794. DANCE, George. Pencil drawing in two variations; **a:** 10″×7½″; **b:** (faintly painted over) 10¼″×7¾″.
Drawn by Dance in London presumably for his own purposes. Version **a:** unsigned, with the inscription 'Dr. Haydn' appears to be the sketch. ⟨Dance Estate; → [1957, London, auction by Sotheby & Co. →] Vienna, Mus. d. Stadt, at present in the Haydn-Museum.⟩ Version **b:** signed 'March 20th, 1794 / Geo: Dance'. ⟨→ London, Royal College of Music.⟩ A third version (right profile) may have served as a pattern for the engraving by W. Daniell (1809). (Landon SofJH, Suppl.: in the possession of Edward Croft-Murray, Richmond.) *Cf.* texts **N, P.**

**12** 179..? Unsigned (ZITTERER, Johann). Gouache, oval: 9½″×7″. Origin unknown. Painted between 1791 and 1800, perhaps in 1795 in Vienna (?). (In 1791 Haydn composed the *Surprise* Symphony [Hoboken I: 94], the second movement of which is in the picture; in 1800 the engraving was published with the note *Peint par Zitterer / Gravé par J. Neidl* by Artaria in Vienna [= Picture Appendix **i**]). The presentation resembles Guttenbrunn's picture (**8**). *Cf.* texts **H, P.** ⟨? Artaria & Co.; → ? → J. Hupka, Wien; → Vienna, Mus. d. Stadt, at present in the Haydn-Museum.⟩— The miniature allegedly lost during World War II (at one time in the possession of E. Volkmann, Leipzig; see Picture Appendix **h**) was presumably only a (contemporary?) copy.

**13** 1799. RÖSLER (ROESLER etc.), Johann Carl. Oil painting, 25″×20½″. Commission unknown.

Dated 'Wien / 1799'; on the back a note by Fr. Rochlitz in German: '...painted in Vienna from life and after formal sittings of the master by Rösler in 1799, shortly after Haydn's second stay in London, and so much like him that I who had shortly before talked to him when he passed through Leipzig recognized him at first glance before I had any idea whom the picture was supposed to present.' *Cf.* also text **R.** ⟨? → Rochlitz; → Felix Mendelssohn-Bartholdy; → his granddaughter; → Oxford, Univ. Faculty of Music.⟩—The pastel first attributed to A. Graff and then to D. Caffé [= Picture Appendix **g**] appears to have been painted not from the model, but copied from Rösler's portrait.

**14** 1799. Unsigned (KININGER, Vincenz Georg). Sepia drawing on paper, oval: 4″×3½″.

Drawn in Vienna to the order of the publishers Breitkopf & Härtel, making use of the Guttenbrunn picture (**8**), however, this is to be considered an independent presentation. The head was pasted on later. *Cf.* texts **K, OPQ**, see also Picture Appendix **b.** ⟨? Breitkopf & Härtel; → ? → 1964: Hans Swarowsky, Vienna; → Staatsbibl. der Stiftung Preuss. Kulturbesitz, Berlin.⟩— Concerning the engraving after Kininger's earlier (lost?) drawing (found to be not applicable) see picture Appendix **c.**

**\*15** 1799. GRASSI, Anton. Plaster bust, without wig, life-size. Lost, see **15a, 15b.** Made in Vienna. *Cf.* texts **KLM, O, S.** (See also **21** !)

**15a, 15b** 1802—. GRASSI, Anton. Bust with wig, unglazed porcelain. **a:** with the inscription *Blandus au-*

*ritas fidibus canoris ducer quercus*, about 16″ high; **b:** with the inscription 'Haydn', about 6″ high.

Version **a** signed and dated 1802; allegedly Haydn sat once again for the sculptor in December 1801 (*cf.* text **S**), the features may be essentially identical with **\*15.** *Cf.* also text **KL.** In the list of Haydn's estate: ...*69. Joseph Haÿdn in Porzelainerde.* ...*76. Joseph Haydn's Büste aus Porzelainerde von Grassÿ, legiert dem Herrn Grafen v. Harrach* [...69. Joseph Haydn in porcelain. ...76. Joseph Haydn's bust made from porcelain by Grassy, left to his lordship Count Harrach]. ⟨Version **b:** →Vienna, Mus. d. Stadt.⟩

**16** About 1800. Unsigned lead bust (with wig), life-size.

Attributed to A. Grassi (*cf.* text **M**: see also the alleged authorship by Thaler). List of Haydn's estate: ...*77. [Joseph Haydn's Büste] dto aus Bleÿ auf Postament* [...77. [Joseph Haydn's bust] dto from lead on pedestal]. ⟨Haydn; →Harrach family; →Wien; Harrach-Galerie [on a modern pedestal].⟩ Concerning the later application for Haydn's monument in Rohrau see text **Y.**

**17a, 17b** About 1800. Unsigned (THALER [THALLER], Franz). Wax bust with vestment and wig, naturalistically painted. **a:** lost; **b:** with pedestal, 11½″ high.

Origin unknown. Version **a** was kept by Haydn in his home. List of Haydn's estate: ... *71. [Joseph Haydn] detto als Wachsbüste unter Glassturz von Thaler* [...71. [Joseph Haydn] detto as wax bust glazed, by Thaler]. ⟨Haydn; → ? → Haslinger; → Dr. Steger, Vienna; → Wien,

Mus. d. Stadt, where the bust was destroyed during World War II. Photo: Vienna ÖNB, Mus. d. Stadt.⟩ Version **b**: Vestment allegedly from pieces of Haydn's own clothes, wig of his own hair. ⟨? → Prince Clemens Metternich; → (1836) Physician Dominik von Vivenot; → Vienna, Kunsthist. Mus.⟩

**18** 180..? ROBATZ, August. Marble bust (without wig), life-size.
Commission unknown. On the back: *von Au. Robatz verf. nach der Natur* [Made by Au. Robatz after nature]. ⟨→ Vienna, GdMF.⟩

**19** 1803. IRRWOCH (IHRWACH, etc.), Sebastian. Wax medallion (right profile), $3\frac{1}{2}''$ in diameter.
Presumably made in Vienna, commissioned by Frederik Samuel Silverstolpe before his return to Sweden. The specimen at present in the possession of the Silverstolpe family is signed: 'Irwach sc. 1803 / Vienna'. A specimen was in Haydn's possession. List of Haydn's estate: ...70. [*Joseph Haydn*] *detto in Wachs poussirt von Irwach* [...70. [Joseph Haydn] detto made from wax by Irwach]; Schnerich mentions another specimen earlier in the possession of Josef Hüttenbrenner; Thieme-Becker *(Allg. Lex. der bild. Künstler)* mentions a further specimen 'in the possession of the widow of the sculptor Heinr. Natter in Vienna'. One of these pieces may be the lost, unsigned medallion variation (repeatedly published, incl. by Marcel) [= Picture Appendix **e**], the duplicated photographic reproduction in left profile of which was published in the 19th century by Simon, Berlin [= Picture Appendix **f**, also the head

only, in right profile, in the introduction]. The engraving variation reprinted among other places in the Dies biography [= Picture Appendix **d**] is closer to the Silverstolpe or another, unknown, version. *Cf.* also texts **KL, T.**

**20** 1805/6. NEUGASS, Isidor. Oil painting, $55'' \times 70''$ (?).
Painted on commission for an Esterházy Scholarship (*cf.* text **U**, there the possible date 1801 of the half-length portrait by Neugass); signed: 'J. Neugass 1805'. ⟨→ Prince Esterházy; → Vienna, Esterházy Palace.⟩

**21** 1808. Unsigned (WEISS, David). Engraving (publ. in 1808 by Artaria & Co., Vienna), oval: $6'' \times 4\frac{1}{2}''$.
From one of the busts in antique style (presumably *15) engraved to the order of the publishing house Artaria; in the absence of a model this may be considered as an independent painting. See also notes to text **O.**

**22** 1808. WIGAND, Balthasar. Performance of Haydn's *Creation* on the 27th March 1808 in the Assembly Hall of the old University of Vienna. Watercolour on the lid of a box, $9'' \times 13\frac{1}{2}''$.
Painted to the order of Princess Maria Josepha Esterházy and presented to

Haydn (*cf.* text **V**); the features of the master sitting in the middle cannot be recognized. ⟨Haydn; → Princess Esterházy; → Franz (Ferenc) Liszt; → Haslinger; → Vienna, Mus. d. Stadt, where it was destroyed during World War II. Photograph: Vienna, ÖNB.⟩

**23** 1809. Death-mask. Modelled by Johann Elssler from gypsum on the advice of A. Ch. Dies and preserved in a mould taken by the Viennese sculptor Anton Fernkorn.
⟨→ Vienna, Mus. d. Stadt, at present in the Haydn-Museum.⟩ See text **K.**

## SUPPLEMENT

**24** 1800 or 1801. DARCIS, Louis (after a lost drawing by Pierre-Narcis GUÉRIN). Engraving (publ. by Pleyel, Paris).
Haydn wished to supply a model (*cf.* texts **HI**); the engraving was presumably made in Paris after **14.**

**25** 1801. GATTEAUX, Nicolas-Marie. Medal, one side of the Paris Medal (bronze and gold, respectively).
A copy of the medal was in Haydn's estate. Made in Paris, not from life, (probably after **14 → 24;** *cf.* notes to the texts **HI**).

**26** 1800? Anonymous pastel.
This was kept in the Esterházy Collection, and s, according to tradition, a portrait of J. Haydn. If it was in fact painted from life, it must be described as an unsuccessful picture from Haydn's last years. *Cf.* also notes to picture No. 363, page 235.

Texts **A–Y**

**A** Haydn's letter to Artaria, 27 May, 1781
[GBA No. 33; CCLN p. 28.]

*...P.S. Sehr vielle freuen sich auf mein Portrait. Das Gemählde schicken Sie mir in dem nemblichen Verschlägl zurück.*
[...P. S. Many people are delighted with my portrait. Return the oil portrait to me in the same box.]

**B** Haydn's letter to Artaria, 23 June, 1781
[GBA No. 34; CCLN pp. 29–30.]

*...Das gemahlen samt den 12 beygefügten sehr schön gestochenen Portrait hab ich mit ausnehmenden Vergnügen erhalten. Ein noch weit grösseres aber fühlt mein gnädigster Fürst, indem da Er solches inne geworden, alsogleich von mir Eines abforderte. Nachdem nun diese 12 Stück nicht hinlänglich, Ersuche ich Euer Hoch Edlen mir um meine Bezahlung noch 6 Stück zu schicken... Sobald ich nach Wien komen solte werden Euer Hoch Edl die liebe für mich haben und mich bey dem so Verdienstvollen Herrn v. Mansfeld aufzuführen. Übrigens sage verbundensten Dank für die überschickten Exemplar und die übrigen Portraits, ...*
[... I received with the greatest pleasure the oil-portrait together with the twelve copies you enclosed of the beautifully engraved portrait. My gracious Prince, however, was even more delighted, for as soon as his attention was drawn to it, he immediately asked me to give him one. Since these 12 copies are not enough, I would ask you, good Sir, to send me another six at my expense... As soon as I come to Vienna, will you be kind enough, good Sir, to present me to the worthy Herr von Mansfeld? Meanwhile I thank you for the copies and the other portraits...]

**C** Haydn's letter to Artaria, 20 July, 1781
[GBA No. 35; CCLN p. 31.]

*...Für die überschickte Portraits machen Sie mich neuerdings zum Schuldner; ob aber solche abgehen? ist eine Neugierde. Durch jene, so Sie mir überschück-*

*ten, hatten bishero Bildhauer und Vergolter Gewinnst...*
[...You once again make me your debtor for the portraits you sent; but do they sell? I'm curious. In any event the frame-makers and guilders have profited by those you sent to me...]

**D** Haydn's letter to Artaria,
18 October, 1781
[GBA No. 38a; CCLN p. 32.]

*...bitte um etwelche Portraits von mir.*
[... Please send me some more of my portraits.]
*Cf.* **2.** The publication of the engraving was announced in the *Wiener Zeitung* of 18. 5. 1781 (Artaria–Botstiber, 14). It is clear from texts **A** and **B** that Mansfeld did not know Haydn personally and used as his model an oil painting [*Gemählde*] sent by Haydn. The picture returned *in dem nemblichen Verschlägl* [in the same box] was presumably a nowadays unknown, lost, and probably small portrait. The engraving bears no resemblance to the Grundmann picture (**1**), which could have been borrowed from Eszterháza with the Prince's permission—in which case it would have been right to retain also the uniform of the Prince's musicians. Should it be possible to date Guttenbrunn's small oil painting (**8**) as from the 1770s (*Cf.* notes to texts **EF**), it could hardly have served as a model for Mansfeld in view of the different features.

**E** Haydn's First London Notebook,
Fol. 28a
*Mahler: Mr. Ott und Guttenbrun.*
[Painters: Mr. Ott and Guttenbrun.]

**F** Haydn's Second London Notebook,
Fol. 28b

*Hardy. Otto. Guttenbrun. Hoppener. Daßie wax posirt. NB: die Ersteren 4 Herrn mahlten mein Portrait. Deßie in wachs.*
[Hardy. Otto. Guttenbrun. Hoppener. Dassie, em-

bossed in wax. N. B.: The first 4 gentlemen painted my portrait, Dessie in wax.]

*Cf.* *7, 8, resp. 10a, *7, 8, 9; the wax medallion by 'Dassie' (= Desoie?) is lost, the last trace of it is a mention by Schnerich 238 ('Half-length portrait by Desoin, London, 1844', probably a copy).—No. 8, painting by Guttenbrunn: Doubts about the earlier dating of the picture around 1770 (which by the way was not supported by any decisive document) in the Haydn iconography are based above all on these two notes. Concerning the value of Haydn's note: 1) About 1789–1795 Ludwig Guttenbrunn worked in fact in London; 2) From his painting (which according to Thieme-Becker, *Allg. Lex. d. bild. Künstler*, originated in 1791) L. Schiavonetti published in 1792 in London an engraving, as did also Bartolozzi (No. 7a) from Ott's miniature (No. *7), and Hardy (No. 10b) from his own painting (No. 10a); 3) Comments of this kind in Haydn's Notebooks refer to events of the time. A comparison of the London pictures Nos. 7–10 does not offer any further evidence. Although the wig is similar in all pictures, the clothes show an essential difference in each. The posture shows an interesting similarity: the creative master with his quill, replaced in Hardy's picture only by a volume of notes (but again the obligatory piano stands in the background). Incidentally, if Guttenbrunn had painted it before the London journey, then, in view of certain biographical data, this must have occurred between 1770 and 1772. Guttenbrunn went to Italy in 1772 and could only have met Haydn again in 1791. It is known that Guttenbrunn painted a portrait of Prince Nikolaus Esterházy 'the Magnificent' in 1770, and participated in the interior decoration of the Palace at Eszterháza. It is conceivable that in a portrait of Haydn which he may have painted at this time he could have portrayed Haydn in uniform, as Grundmann had also done in picture No. 1. It cannot be denied that in the painting by Guttenbrunn Haydn looks rather young; this, however, could be artistic 'agelessness', since the engraving from Ott's picture (No. 7a, 1791) does not depict Haydn any older, either; so that this does not refute the date 1791. However, the existence of the two Guttenbrunn versions admits the hypothesis that the more sketchy No. 8a may have originated at Eszterháza at the beginning of the 1770s, but No. 8b was made in London as a more elaborate model for the engraver. It is, however, more likely that both paintings were completed in London, and version No. 8a was either 1) a first version, or 2) a copy for Haydn himself, which he brought home, and which was kept and venerated by his wife (since 'Guttenbrunn had been her lover', comp. text O).

**G** HAYDN'S LETTER TO FRAU VON GENZINGER, 20 DECEMBER, 1791
[GBA No. 167; CCLN p. 123.]

*...Der Printz v. Wallis läst mich nun abmahlen, und das Portrait wird in seinem Cabinet aufgemacht...*
[... The Prince of Wales is having my portrait painted just now, and the picture is to hang in his room...]

*Cf.* 9. A further relevant entry in Haydn's Second London Notebook, Fol. 13A; *der Prince Wallis verlangte mein Portrait* [the Prince of Wales asked for my portrait].—'It is said that one day, Haydn, making himself ready to go to Hoppner, looked uneasily into the mirror and said peevishly: *Ich sehe heute nicht gut aus, ich werde nicht zu Hrn. Hoppner gehen* [I am not looking well today, I shall not go to Mr. Hoppner].' (Pohl: *Mozart und Haydn in London*, p. 167.)—The privately commissioned oil painting may have been first published as an engraving in 1807 (by Georg Sigismund Facius).

**H** HAYDN'S LETTER TO ARTARIA, 3 SEPTEMBER, 1800
[GBA No. 252; CCLN p. 175.]

*...da ich aber wünschte Ihme [Pleyel] meines Portraits wegen gefällig zu werden, so gelanget meine bitte an Sie meine Herrn, Ihme in Nahmen meiner einen abdruck von den vielleicht schon verfertigten sehr guten Portraits, so ich lezthin bey Sie gesehen nach Dresden zu schücken, damit er es darnach in das kleinere Copiren und denen quartetten beydrucken köne...*
[...But I want to oblige him [Pleyel] about my portrait, and so I would ask you, gentlemen, to send to Dresden, in my name, a pull of the very good portrait which I saw at your office last time, and which is perhaps published by now. He will copy it and publish it in a reduced size...]

**I** HAYDN'S LETTER TO PLEYEL, 4 MAY, 1801
[GBA No. 264; CCLN pp. 179–180.]

*... Je voudrais bien savoir quand paraîtra ta belle édition de mes quatuors, et si tu as, oui ou non, reçu par Artaria l'exemplaire de ma Création, ainsi que mon portrait; ...*
[...I would very much like to know when your beautiful edition of my Quartets will appear, and whether or not you have received the copy of my *Creation* and also the portrait which Artaria sent to you...]

*Cf.* 12, 24. The text **H** must refer to the engraving made by Johann Neidl from Zitterer's picture (12) (in 1800, at Artaria, Vienna, see Picture Appendix i). The other quotation, see text **I**, lacks concrete date, but it can be presumed that it concerns the above-mentioned engraving. But the engraving made by N. Darcis from the drawing by Guérin (24), in the *Collection Complette des Quatuors*, is not a copy of the Zitterer-Neidl engraving. Concerning the origin of picture 24, we offer the following hypothesis. In 1800 Pleyel probably received in Dresden or from the orderer, the firm Breitkopf & Härtel, the Kininger picture (14) or one of the engravings made from the latter. (Engraving by C. Pfeiffer: 1800, on the title-page of Breitkopf & Härtel's edition of *Œuvres Complettes* Vol. I.; Engraving by H. Schmidt: 1800, Leipzig [see Picture Appendix b].) It is confirmed in AmZ, 6. 10. 1800, Col. 40 that the publishing house of Breitkopf & Härtel negotiated with Pleyel and obtained the distribution rights for Pleyel's Complete Edition of Haydn's quartets for Germany. Because of the late arrival of the picture promised by Haydn, Pleyel should have handed Guérin the Kininger portrait in Paris. If this had been negotiated by Breitkopf & Härtel, Guérin should not have it simply copied, but would only have used it as a model for a new picture. While keeping some characteristic features, Guérin changed the perspective oddly. It should be noted that the head of

Haydn on Gatteaux's medallion (**25**) was also modelled from **14,** or after the drawing by Guérin from the latter. This appears to be confirmed by several details of the features. It is obvious that Gatteaux, who had never seen Haydn, could not avoid some mistakes as he changed the angle of the profile, e.g. the projecting part of the chin, which is clearly protruding on Kininger's and is still well discernible on the similar Guérin–Darcis picture, has lost much of its character with Gatteaux. Further data about the Gatteaux medallion are to be found in the AmZ of 16th September 1801, News from Paris, Col. 839: 'The medallion has been made from a portrait resembling Haydn, which was ordered from Germany',—in Griesinger 41 who characterized the medal as 'a lifelike portrait bust of Haydn', and in Dies 180, who simply mentioned the picture.

**K** GRIESINGER [GRASBERGER ED.: PP. 51–52; GOTWALS ED.: PP. 51–52].

*Die besten Büsten von Haydn sind unstreitig die, welche sein Freund, der geschickte Modellier bei der Wiener-Porzellanfabrik, Herr Grassy (sein Tod am 30sten Dec. 1807. fiel Haydn äußerst empfindlich) nach dem Leben verfertigt hat. Die eine ist in natürlicher Grösse und antiker Form mit der Aufschrift:*

> *Tu potis tigres comitesque sylvas*
> *Ducere, et currentes rivos morari.*

*Die andere, in kleinerem Maßstabe, stellt Haydn mit der Perücke und in seiner gewöhnlicher Kleidung vollkommen ähnlich dar, und Grassy setzte darunter:*

> *Blandus auritas fidibus canoris ducere quercus.*

*Zum sprechen getroffen sind auch die Bilder von Haydn, welche ein Graveur, namens Irwasch, zu Wien in Wachs als Cameen verfertigte. Unter den mir bekannten Kupferstichen ist der bey Breitkopf und Härtel in Leipzig erschienene, obschon nicht ganz getreu, doch der beste. Johann Elssler, achtzehn Jahre hindurch Haydns Kopist und treuer Diener, liess den Kopf seines Herrn nach seinem Tod in Gips abformen. Lavater, der jeden Schattenriß in seiner Sammlung mit einem Vers characterisiert, schrieb unter Haydns Bild:*

> *Etwas mehr als Gemeines erblick' ich im Aug'*
> *und der Nase;*
> *Auch die Stirn ist gut; im Munde 'was vom Philister.*

*Die starke, durch ihr Gewicht etwas herunterhängende Unterlippe mag dieses Urtheil veranlaßt haben.*

[The best busts of Haydn are unquestionably those that his friend, the capable modeler at the Vienna Porcelain Works, Herr Grassi (Haydn took his death on December 30, 1807, very hard) made from life. One of them is life-size in the antique manner with the inscription:

> *Tu potis tigres comitesque sylvas*
> *Ducere, et currentes rivos morari.*
> (Thou canst lead beasts and companion forests
> And still the flowing streams.
> Horace, *Odes*, III, xi.)

The other, smaller in scale, portrays Haydn perfectly in wig and customary clothing, and Grassi placed below it:

> *Blandus auritas fidibus canoris ducere quercus.*
> (And blandish the listening oaks with singing strings.
> Horace, *Odes*, I, xii.)]

Also of speaking likeness are the pictures of Haydn that an engraver named Ihrwach made in Vienna as wax cameos. Among the engravings known to me, the one at Breitkopf & Härtel in Leipzig appears to be the best, though not entirely faithful. Johann Elssler, for eighteen years Haydn's copyist and faithful servant, had a plaster cast of his master's head made after his death. Lavater, who characterized every silhouette in his collection with a verse, wrote under Haydn's portrait:

> Something more than the ordinary I perceive in the
> eye and the nose;
> The forehead too is good; in the mouth somewhat
> philistine.

The strong, somewhat heavy lower lip may have given rise to this opinion.]

*Cf.* **\*15, 15a, 19, 14** (engraving variation), **23** and **6** (?). The engraving published at Breitkopf & Härtel from Kininger is due to Griesinger's efforts (see below), and it is therefore not surprising that he should prefer it to other engravings. The silhouette in the Lavater collection may be identical with **6** or one of its variations. (Rosemary Hughes described the silhouette as Lavater's work; see: *Haydn*, London, 1950).

**L** DIES (SEEGER ED.: P. 11; GOTWALS ED.: P. 75.)

*Anton Grassi, Bildhauer (Bruder des Joseph Grassi, Hofmalers und Professors zu Dresden) und Modellmeister bei der k. k. Porzellanfabrik in Wien. Er verfertigte Haydns lebensgrosse und sehr ähnliche Büste und starb am 1. Januar 1808.—Auch Herr Ihrwach lieferte ein äußerst ähnliches Medaillon.*

[Anton Grassi, sculptor (brother of Joseph Grassi, court painter and professor at Dresden) and master pattern-maker at the Imperial Porcelain Works in Vienna. He made a life-size and very faithful bust of Haydn, and died on January 1, 1808. Herr Irrwoch also struck a medal of uncommon likeness.]

*Cf.* **\*15, 19.** A. Grassi was a friend of Dies, who had introduced him to Haydn. It is curious that thr landscape painter Dies did not describe the othee Haydn p ortraits which were in the master's house

**M** DIES (FROM DESCRIPTION OF HAYDN'S SECOND WILL)

*49. Paragraph: 'Vermache ich dem Herrn Grafen von Harrach, Herrn der Herrschaft Rohrau, die kleine goldene Medaille von Paris mit dem dazugehörigen Brief des Amateurs der Musik nebst der großen Büste à l'antique' (Haydn's Büste von A. Grassi).*

[§ 49. 'I bequeath to Count Harrach, Lord of the Rohrau domain, the little gold medal from Paris, with teh accompanying letter from the *Amateurs* of music; also the large bust *à l'antique*' (Haydn's bust by A. Grassi).]

*Cf.* **16** or **\*15**? The reference in parentheses was added by Dies. According to Botstiber, the text of the will referred to Grassi's bust (**\*15**, which according to his information was acquired by the GdMF and was lost later). The list of Haydn's estate mentions a *Büste aus porzelainerde von Grassi* [bust of porcelain by Grassi], (i.e. a Grassi bust not *à l'antique*, as e.g. **15a** or **15b**?), which he had left to Count Harrach. In fact, however, it was the unsigned lead bust (**16**) that as a result of Haydn's will entered the possession of the Harrach family, where it has been kept to his day. (See also text **Y**; the same lead bust served as a model for the Haydn monument erected in the 1840s in Rohrau.) The addition of *à l'antique*—or according to the autograph, *en Antike*—appears undoubteeds to refer to the lost bust by Grassi, *15, nor do the classicizing clothes of the lead bust with wig exclude the attribute en Antike. Supposing that the reference in Haydn's will referred to the lead bust (and Dies himself was of this opinion), this place in Dies's book would be almost the only evidence to attribute it to Grassi. (Cf. also text O.) The surviving variations of Grassi's bust of Haydn (15a, 15b) differ so conspicuously from the lead bust that the ascription to Grassi seems doubtful.—Franz Thaller (the likely sculptor of Haydn's wax bust, 17), who made numerous metal and bronze busts in Vienna around 1800, may also be considered as the creator of the lead bust. This supposition can be justified from an artistic point of view, as the pock-marks on the face are most conspicuous in the 16 and 17 statues.

**N** POHL–BOTSTIBER, 30 (GRIESINGER'S LETTER TO BREITKOPF & HÄRTEL, 12 JUNE, 1799)

*...Haydn ist mit den Portraits, welche man im Publicum verkauft, nicht zufrieden: dreymal sey er in England gestochen worden, Eines habe Bartolozzi selbst corrigiert, es sey aber keines recht getroffen. Besser sey ein Gemählde von Gutenbronn, welches er einem seiner Bekannten zum Abzeichnen gegeben habe. Das beste sey in Profil von einem Engländer Danz (so sprach wenigstens Haydn aus), einem sehr guten Kopfe, welches er alle Tage aus England erwarte und zum Nachstechen vor Ihre Ausgabe seiner Clavierkompositionen gerne geben wolle...*

[...Haydn is not satisfied with the portraits which are being sold to the public; he was engraved three times in England, and one of them was corrected by Bartolozzi himself, but it is not a good likeness. The painting by Gutenbronn, which he gave for drawing to one of his acquaintances, is said to be better. The best profile is said to be by an Englishman called Danz (at least Haydn said so), a very good head, which he expects from England any day and which he wishes to give you for engraving for your edition of his Compositions for Piano...]

*Cf. *7, 7a, 8, 11* and Picture Appendix **a**
The picture 'corrected by Bartolozzi himself' is the lost painting by Ott (*7); Guttenbrunn's painting was engraved by Luigi Schiavonetti in London in 1792; Dance's drawing was multiplied as an engraving only in 1809 in London (by William Daniell in the series 'Collection of Portraits sketched from the life since 1793 by George Dance', 1807–1814). It is hard to understand why Haydn did not mention the engraving by Hardy (**10b**).

**O** POHL–BOTSTIBER, PP. 153–154.

*From Griesinger's letters of this period (1799) we obtain valuable disclosures about the portraits of Haydn which were produced at the time. Breitkopf and Härtel... had a drawing of Gutenbrunn's picture made by Vincenz Georg Kinninger. Nobody was satisfied with this drawing and Kinninger should have drawn it again from Gutenbrunn's portrait. But the picture was taken to Baden by Frau Haydn, who would not give it up again, because 'Gutenbrunn war ehemals, sagte Haydn, ihr Liebhaber, und daher trennt sie sich so selten als möglich von dem Porträt' ['Gutenbrunn, Haydn said, had once been her lover, and so she parted with the portrait as seldom as possible']. Griesinger suggested that Kinninger should make a drawing from Haydn's bust which had been modelled a short time*

*earlier from nature by Grassi (Griesinger wrote 'Grasset'), the best modeller and artistic director of the imperial porcelain factory of Vienna. Only one cast of this bust existed, and Grassi hesitated whether to make further ones from porcelain, because the all-powerful Count Saurau had promised him to induce the Emperor or the Empress to have the bust cast from metal. But Grassi had a small number of medallions made from this bust, one of which Griesinger sent to Breitkopf & Härtel, with the following comment: 'Was nur die Ähnlichkeit betrifft, so ist sie in diesem Abdrucke gewis getroffen, besonderst ist die untere fleischige und massive Lippe charakteristisch. Die gutmütigen Züge welche sich in Haydns Gesicht entfalten, so bald er spricht, seine braune und blatternarbige Haut, das volle Aug, die Perrücke—liessen sich freilich auf diesem antiken Kopf nicht darstellen, aber auch nur das fehlt, um ihn gleich zu erkennen.' ['As far as likeness is concerned, it is certainly good in this copy; the fleshy and massive lower lip is especially characteristic. The traits of good-nature which Haydn's face displays as soon as he begins to speak, his brown and pock-marked skin, the full eye, the wig—could of course not be shown on this antique head, but except for these, he can be instantly recognized.']*

*Cf. 14 (?), 8, *15* (and the model for **21**?)
Kininger's drawing, which 'nobody was satisfied with', is presumably an earlier version of picture **14** (= Kininger's first version), because the upper part including the head was pasted later to the paper with the sepia drawing, and a new head was fitted into the drawing. The (lost) drawing known from the oval engraving signed 'Kininger d. Wien—Fr. Bolt sc. Berlin 1799' seems to be Kininger's second version. (See Picture Appendix **c**; also with a lyre in the background, doubtless influenced by the Guttenbrunn painting, **8**.) Finally, the third version by Kininger (**14**) served as a model for various German editions of the engraving and was used by the publishers Breitkopf & Härtel for the title-page of Volume I of the Œuvres Complettes.—The (lost) medal by Grassi, described by Griesinger, presumably served as a model for engraving **21**.

**P** POHL–BOTSTIBER, p. 154. (LETTER FROM GRIESINGER TO BREITKOPF & HÄRTEL, 3 JULY, 1799)

*Werthester Freund,
H. Kinninger ist bereit, das Portrait, so wie Sie es verlangen, abzuzeichnen. Mit H. Kohl habe ich noch nicht gesprochen; er ist auf dem Lande.
H. Haydn will mir in drey Tägen das Gutenbrunnsche Portrait zustellen; er befürchtet daß es als Kupferstich einen üblen Effekt machen möchte, indem er in einer Stellung abgemahlt sey, wo er eben an einer Composition studierte. Hierüber müßten nun, wie mich dünkt, die HH. Kinninger und Kohl entscheiden. Auf den Fall, daß sie das Gutenbrunnsche Portrait nicht passend finden, und daß das Danzische nicht bald aus England komme, räht Haydn das von Artaria besorgte urgieren zu lassen, weil viele seiner Bekannten es nicht unähnlich finden...*

[My Esteemed Friend,
Mr. Kinninger is ready to draw the portrait according to your wish. I have not yet talked to Mr. Kohl; he is in the country.
Mr. Haydn will deliver to me Gutenbrunn's portrait

in three days; he is afraid that it would make a bad impression as a copper engraving, because he is painted in a pose as if studying one of his compositions. It seems to me that Messrs. Kinninger and Kohl should decide about this. In case they do not find the portrait by Gutenbrunn suitable, and if Dance's does not arrive from England soon, Haydn advises that you should urge the one ordered from Artaria, as many of his acquaintances find that it is not unlike him...]

*Cf.* **14, 8, 11, 12.** The portrait 'ordered from Artaria' is assumed to be the engraving by J. Neidl [=Picture Appendix **i**] from the gouache by Zitterer (**12**).

**Q** Pohl–Botstiber, p. 155. (Letter from Griesinger to Breitkopf & Härtel, 20 July, 1799)

*...H. Haydn ist zu dem Fürsten Esterhazy nach Eisenstadt in Ungarn gereist, und seine Frau, eine gute alte Matrone, hielt mich einige Zeit hin, bis sie das Gutenbrunnsche Portrait von einer ihrer Bekannten abholen, und mir zustellen ließ. Es scheint mir sehr ähnlich, Haydns Frau hält es für das beste, und H. Kinninger, dem ich es sogleich übergab, ist auch damit zufrieden. Er wird in höchstens vierzehn Tagen mit der Zeichnung fertig seyn und sie dem H. John zum Stechen übergeben, weil er glaubt, daß John's Manier eleganter, und netter als die Kohl'sche ist...* [...Mr. Haydn has gone to Prince Esterházy's at Eisenstadt in Hungary, and his wife, a good old lady, put me off for some time before she allowed one of her acquaintances to fetch Gutenbrunn's portrait and deliver it to me. It seems to be a good likeness, Haydn's wife holds it to be the best, and Mr. Kinninger, to whom I gave it at once, is also satisfied with it. He will have finished the drawing in fourteen days at the latest and give it to Mr. John for engraving, because he believes that John's style is smarter and neater than Kohl's...]

*Cf.* **8, 14.**

**R** Pohl–Botstiber, p. 152.

*In mid-September [1799] the painter Roesler goes to Eisenstadt and will stay there for about a month. Although Rosenbaum, who mentioned the painter Roesler several times in his Notes, did not report that Haydn had his portrait painted then, it is nevertheless to be assumed that the oil painting by Roesler (unfortunately lost) which was later frequently copied by engravers, was painted then. Rosenbaum mentioned only Roesler painting the younger Tomasini.*

*Cf.* **13.** Since the unsigned pastel picture ⟨→ Musik-bibl. der Stadt Leipzig, see Picture Appendix **g**⟩ appears to be closely linked with Rösler's painting (**13**), and since the detailed painting does not seem to be a copy of the less detailed pastel, and since the Rösler painting is proved to be authentic, one may refrain from the inclusion of the pastel in the list of authentic Haydn portraits. The counter-arguments —1) a note on the back of the picture in the hand of its owner (Alfred Grenser, Wien, 1875!): Joseph Haydn..., painted in pastels by Dresden court painter Anton Graff...; 2) Botstiber: 'Allegedly painted in Dresden in 1795 on Haydn's return journey from London'—are held by us to be insufficient. Vogel (p. 21) attributed the picture to Daniel Caffé, on stylistic grounds.

**S** Pohl–Botstiber, p. 395.

*In December 1801 the sculptor Grassi modelled two busts of Haydn, one larger and one smaller. Haydn sat for Grassi for both. Five of each were ordered from England; they were busts made from white bisque. A few years earlier Grassi had modelled a life-size bust of Haydn which showed him in antique costume; the later one showed him in contemporary clothes, with his wig.* *Cf.* **15a, 15b.**

**T** Pohl–Botstiber, p. 221.

*A wax medallion of Haydn by Irrwoch probably dates from the same period [1803]. According to Neukomm's and Dies's notes, the medallion, in two sittings, was considered by everybody as Haydn's best likeness.*

*Cf.* **19.** Dies, who came to know Haydn in 1805, could not have seen the specimen of Silverstolpe (who was recalled to Sweden in 1803). Perhaps he mentioned that (lost?) copy which is reproduced in the Picture Appendix **e.**

**U** Pohl–Botstiber, p. 251.

*In the years 1805–1806, a young painter, Isidor Neugass, completed a picture of Haydn, which he handed to Prince Esterházy. The Prince paid him 500 florins and granted him a scholarship of 50 florins per month to continue his education.* [*Footnote:*][1] *... On the picture itself the dating reads: Peint par I. Neugass 1805 [Painted by I. Neugass 1805]. The painter's letter of request for the acceptance of his painting is dated 7 December, 1806.*

*Cf.* **20.** Concerning a copy of the picture (a half-length portrait only) see Geiringer II (as 'painting by Neugass, 1801'!). According to a Neugass researcher (György Rózsa, Budapest) this smaller picture was made before picture No. **20**; this, however, has to be proved yet.

**V** Pohl–Botstiber, p. 267.

*Joh. Fr. Reichardt, who arrived in Vienna on 24th November, 1808, wrote: '...Then a female attendant brought all kinds of beautiful, and partly valuable things. The most interesting among them was a rather large flat box, which had been ordered for our Haydn by the Princess Esterházy, the wife of the Prince now reigning, son of Haydn's life-long master. It was made of black ebony, heavily gilded and decorated with gold reliefs. The lid was painted with the movingly beautiful scene in the Akademiesaal, the last great performance of Haydn's Creation, which turned into a real apotheosis for the artist.'* *Cf.* **22.**

**W** Pohl I, p. 219.

*We have to think of him in uniform, in light-blue tails with silver braids and buttons, the waistcoat also light blue, with embroidered frills and necktie. He is shown thus in an oil painting completed probably towards the end of the sixties (probably by Grundmann) at Eszter-háza, which flattered him strongly however. His description handed down by word of mouth is much better* matched by a painting on wood, from around 1770 by J. A. Gutenbrunn, which was published as an outstanding engraving (in Punktirmanier by Luigi Schiavonetti in London and in lithograph by Paterno in Vienna).

Cf. **1, 8.** Concerning the painting by Guttenbrunn see the annotations to the texts **EF.**

**X** POHL, I, PP. 182–183.

The portrait included in this volume comes from the second half of the eighties. The original miniature, to which a curl of Haydn's hair is also attached, is a watercolour on ivory, and was earlier in the possession of Frau Josefa Freiin von Erggelet, b. von Henikstein, who had received it from Haydn's own hands.

Cf. **5.**

**Y** POHL–BOTSTIBER, P. 99.

The lyre crowning the monument [to Haydn in Rohrau] was later replaced by a plaster bust of Haydn, and when the latter too fell victim to the weather, by a sandstone bust. The latter was made in Vienna by the sculptor Procop in the forties, after a metal bust in the Harrach Castle, which Haydn had bequeathed to Count Harrach, and which he himself is said to have described as his closest likeness.

Cf. **16.** The monument stands near the church in Rohrau.

**a** L. Schiavonetti.
Engraving after
Guttenbrunn (publ.
1792, London), see **8**.
14″×11″

**b** (left) H. Schmidt.
Engraving after
Kininger (publ. 1800,
Leipzig), see **14**.
5½″×4″

**c** (right) Fr. Bolt.
Engraving after
Kininger (publ. 1799,
Berlin), see **14** and
text **O**

(LEFT, FROM TOP TO
BOTTOM:)

d D. WEISS. ENGRAVING
AFTER IRRWOCH (PUBL.
1810, VIENNA), SEE **19**

e UNSIGNED, LOST (?)
MEDAL BY IRRWOCH,
SEE **19**

f MEDAL BY IRRWOCH,
REPRODUCED BY PHOTO
SIMON, BERLIN, SEE **19**

(RIGHT, FROM TOP TO
BOTTOM:)

g UNSIGNED PASTEL
PICTURE IN THE
POSSESSION OF THE
MUSIKBIBLIOTHEK DER
STADT LEIPZIG, SEE **13**.
14″×10″

h LOST MINIATURE
by J. ZITTERER (?), SEE **12**.
3″ DIAMETER

i J. NEIDL. ENGRAVING
AFTER ZITTERER (PUBL.
1800 AT ARTARIA & CO.,
VIENNA), SEE **12**

# LIST OF SOURCES AND ANNOTATIONS

Page XVIII
Signatures of Haydn from his musical manuscripts.
Left: a) Divertimento, Hoboken II: 16;

b) *La canterina*, Intermezzo, Hoboken XXVIII: 2;

c) 'Da che penso a maritarmi...', inserted aria, Hoboken XXIVb: 16.

Right: d) Symphony, Hoboken I: 35;

e) *Missa in tempore belli*, Hoboken XXII: 9;

f) *'Hungarischer National Marsch'*, Hoboken VIII: 4

(Budapest, Nat. Lib., Music Department Ms. Mus. I. 47, I. 1, I. 15, I. 33, I. 19, I. 43a)

Page XIX
Signatures of Haydn from receipts, files, letters.
Left: a) *Instructio et Conventio Musicorum*, 5. 5. 1762;

b) Document of agreement between Haydn's musicians, Marteau and Pohl, 21. 12. 1771;

c) CCLN p. 241, 12. 1806;

Right:

d) CCLN pp. 6–7, 5. 12. 1766;

e) CCLN p. 238, 17. 8. 1805;

f) CCLN p. 248, 22. 12. 1808.

(a–d and f: Budapest, Nat. Lib., Dept. for Theatrical History A. M. 252, 4, 2227, 53, 2564; e: Artaria–Botstiber.)

Page XXII
Haydn's seal, 1771. Budapest, Nat. Lib., Dept. for Theatrical History A. M. 4 (enlarged).

Page 1
1 Budapest, Nat. Lib., Cartographic Coll.

Page 2
2 Oil by Wilhelm Kröpsch, 1829. Vienna, ÖNB.
3 Geiringer I.
'Joseph Haydn was...', Griesinger 8.—It could not be ascertained whether he was born on the 31st March, but there is no doubt that he was baptized on the 1st April.

Page 3
4 Engraving by Karl Postl. Vienna, ÖNB.
'The father, an ordinary cartwright...', Dies p. 80.

'In his youth...', Dies p. 80.
'My late father...', CCLN p. 19.

Page 4
5 Oil. Vienna, ÖNB.
'One day the headmaster...', Griesinger p. 9.
'Almighty God...', CCLN p. 19.

Page 5
6 Lithograph after Jacob Alt. Budapest, Nat. Mus.
7 Engraving. Budapest, Nat. Mus.

Page 6
8 Engraving by Johann Ziegler, 1780. Budapest Nat. Mus.
'Haydn, who even then...', Griesinger p. 9.

Page 7
9 Drawn and engraved by Karl Schütz, 1782. Budapest, Nat. Mus.
10 Engraving, 1740. Leipzig, Verlagsarchiv.

Pages 8–9
11 Vienna, Kunsthistorisches Museum.

Page 10
12 Engraving from *Beschreibung der Metropolitankirche zu St. Stephan...* [Description of the Metropolitan Church of St. Stephen...], Vienna, 1779. Budapest, Nat. Lib.
'Besides the scant...', Griesinger p. 10.

Page 11
13 Oil. Vienna, Mus. d. Stadt (Photo: Vienna, ÖNB).
'He also came to know...', Griesinger p. 10.
'I admit I had...', quoted by Griesinger p. 10.

Page 12
14 Oil. Vienna, GdMF.
'No instruction in music theory...', Griesinger p. 10.
'Joseph was then already...', Dies p. 87.
'Reutter was...', Dies pp. 86–87.

Page 13
15 Watercolour. Vienna, Mus. d. Stadt (Photo: Vienna, ÖNB).
16 Jančik: Michael Haydn. Vienna, 1952. Amalthea Verlag.

66 Detail from a painting on canvas. Budapest, State Archives.

Page 43

67 Engraving by M. Weinmann, from the 'Description of the Prince's Palace of Eszterháza in the Kingdom of Hungary'. Pressburg, 1784. Budapest, Nat. Mus.

Page 44

68 Engraving from the 'Description...', Budapest, Nat. Mus.

69 Engraving by M. Weinmann, from the 'Description...', Budapest, Nat. Mus.

Page 45

70 Engraving by F. Landerer, from the 'Description...', Budapest, Nat. Mus.

71 Engraving from the 'Description..', Budapest, Nat. Mus.

Pages 46–47

72, 73 From the 'Description...', Budapest, Nat. Lib.

74 Engraving by Joseph von Fernstein, from the 'Description...', Budapest, Nat. Mus.

75 Blueprint. Budapest, State Archives.

Page 48

76 Detail of picture 71.
Poem by Márton Dallos; the original Hungarian text in 'Eszterházi várnak és ához tartozandó nevezetesebb helyeinek rövid leirása...' [Short Description of the Palace of Eszterháza and of the remarkable places belonging to it.] Sopron, 1781. English translation by Mari Kuttna.

Page 49

77–78 Budapest, Nat. Lib., Music Dept. Ms. Mus. I. 2 and Ms. Mus. I. 3.

Page 50

79 See Iconogr. No. 1, p. 213 (Photo: Robert Forstner, Eisenstadt). According to Archivist Johann Harich, Eisenstadt, the original was destroyed in Eszterháza during World War II.

Page 51

80 Budapest, Nat. Lib., Dept. for Theatrical History A. M. 56. Text of the letter: CCLN p. 8.

81 Engraving by Lorenzo Zucchi after C. P. Rotari. Budapest, Nat. Lib.

Page 52

82 Coloured etching. Budapest, Nat. Mus.
'First, I would ask...', CCLN pp. 9–11.

Page 53

83 Budapest, Nat. Lib., Music Dept. Ms. Mus. I. 34. In the improved bars the first violin originally played a figurative, longer version.
'Have you...', Dies p. 109.

Page 54

84 Budapest, Nat. Lib., Music Dept. Ms. Mus. I. 47. The two-page sketch is at the end of the F-major Divertimento Manuscript (Hoboken II: 16).

85 Published 1779. (Coll. Anthony van Hoboken, Ascona.)
'From the quantity...', Griesinger pp. 61–62.

Page 55

86 Vienna, GdMF (Photo: Vienna, ÖNB, PhA).

87 Engraving by Salomon Kleiner. Budapest, Nat. Mus.

N. B. There has been no proof so far that Haydn was acquainted with the music of Handel and Bach in the 1770s. At that time Baron van Swieten—who later initiated the baroque music performances—was Ambassador to Berlin and only spent his holidays in Vienna; regular performances of baroque music in his home began in the 1780s. On stylistic grounds, however, such an influence on Haydn's music around 1772–1773 should be noted. We are excluding that possibility that the German literary school of *Sturm und Drang*, or Goethe's works, had the slightest influence on the non-literary Haydn.

Pages 56–57

88–91 Budapest, Nat. Lib., Music Dept. Ms. Mus. I. 36.
'In Prince Esterházy's orchestra...', Griesinger, p. 19.
'I was then young...', Dies p. 101.

Page 58

92 Engraving by Charles Pechwill, from a painting by Lorenz (properly: Ludwig) Guttenbrunn, 1770. (See pictures 48 and 194.) Budapest, Nat. Mus.
'Most Serene and Noble...', CCLN pp. 15–16.

Page 59

93 Budapest, Nat. Lib., Dept. for Theatrical History.

94 Budapest, Nat. Lib., Dept. for Theatrical History, A. M. 626.

Page 60

95 Engraving by János Berkeny after Szabó and Karl Schütz, 3. 8. 1791, lightly coloured. Budapest, Nat. Mus.

96 From the so-called *Linus* Manuscript, second half of the 18th century, which contains several 'Singar' [Gipsy] Dances similar to Haydn's 'Hungarian' motifs. (Published by Zoltán Falvy in *Zenetudományi Tanulmányok*, Vol. VI, Budapest, 1957). Budapest, Nat. Lib., Music Dept.

97 From the Artaria edition, revised by Haydn, 1800. Budapest, Nat. Lib., Music Dept.

Page 61

98 Detail from another copy of the engraving 95. Budapest, Nat. Mus.

99 'Œuvres Complettes de Joseph Haydn.' Cah. III.. *Klavierstimme* [Part for Piano]. Breitkopf & Härtel, Budapest, Nat. Lib., Music Dept.

100 Manuscript by Haydn. Budapest, Nat. Lib., Music Dept. Ms. Mus. I. 43.

Page 62

101 Rudolf Ludwig: *Schattenrisse aus Österreich*, Vienna, 1912.

102 Engraving. Vienna, ÖNB.

103 Engraving by Quirin Mark. Vienna, ÖNB.

Page 63

104 Munich, Theatermuseum.—Tradition has it that this represents a performance of Haydn's opera *L'incontro improvviso* at Eszterháza in 1775 with Haydn himself directing from the clavier. As we know that numerous operas by other composers on Turkish subjects were also performed at Eszterháza, the date at least appears to be doubtful (*cf.* Horányi, Bartha–Somfai). Some details even indicate some other theatre than Eszterháza. 1) The shape of the Eszterháza stage was square and about 40′ by 40′ (*cf.* picture 74 and see Horányi); yet the gouache shows an oblong stage, appearing to be wider than 40′; 2) The music-desk in the opera at Eszterháza was, as shown by documents, a flat table (kindly suggested by Johann Harich); while the picture shows the front of a slanting, double music-desk. For this reason, this gouache has not been included among the authentic pictures of Haydn.

105 Budapest, Nat. Lib.

106 From the 'Description...', Budapest, Nat. Lib.

107 Engraving by Jacob Schmutzer after de Greux, 1770. Budapest, Nat. Mus.

108 *Bilder-Atlas zur Musikgeschichte von Bach bis Strauss* [The History of Music in Pictures from Bach to Strauss]. Ed. by Gustav Kahnt. Berlin, Schuster & Loeffler.

109 Engraving. Budapest, Nat. Mus. N. B. A receipt in the Est. Arch. confirms that Haydn owned some puppets. (Budapest, Nat. Lib., Dept. for Theatrical History, A. M. 1354; see also Horányi.)

110 Engraving by Johann Neidl after Thomas Hardy. Photo: Coll. H. C. Robbins Landon, Buggiano/Vienna.

111–112 From the Est. Arch., now Budapest, Nat. Lib., Music Dept. Ha. I. 10.

113 Engraving, Vienna, ÖNB.

114–117 Budapest, Nat. Lib., Dept. for Theatrical History, A. M. 4225. (Mildew spots on the paper make it difficult to read the writing.) Text: CCLN pp. 18–20, see there the difference between the various versions of Haydn's famous autobiography.—Haydn partly mis-spells the towns. Two important mistakes: 1) born 1732 (and not 1733), 2) *in gegenwarth Ihro k.k. Majestät* [in the presence of Her Imperial and Royal Majesty], the opera *L'infedeltà delusa* (and not *L'incontro improvviso*) was performed.

118 Engraving by Vischer. Vienna, ÖNB.

119 Engraving by Karl Tuschnitz, Vienna, ÖNB. 'He did not know...', Griesinger p. 17.

120 Engraving after Johann Ziegler. Vienna, ÖNB.

121 Lithograph by Jacob Alt. Budapest, Nat. Lib.

122–123 Budapest, Nat. Lib.

124 Engraving by Marco Pitteri after Gianbattista Piazetta. Vienna, ÖNB.

125 Engraving by Friedrich Wilhelm Bollinger, 1803. Budapest, Nat. Lib., Music Dept.

126 Engraving by H. E. von Wintter, 1817. Vienna, ÖNB.

127 Libretto. Budapest, Nat. Lib.

128–129 Engraving by Johann Gottfried Scheffner. Budapest, Nat. Lib., Music Dept.

130 Budapest, Nat. Lib., Music Dept.

131 Original previously in the Est. Coll. After a photograph. Budapest, Iparművészeti Múzeum [Museum of Applied Arts].

132–133 Budapest, Nat. Lib.

134 From Travaglia's sketches. Budapest, Nat. Lib., Dept. for Theatrical History.

135 Budapest, Nat. Lib.

136–137 See Horányi. Budapest, Nat. Lib., Dept. for Theatrical History.

138 From Travaglia's sketches. Budapest, Nat. Lib.. Dept. for Theatrical History.

139 Detail from a blueprint. Budapest, State Archives.

140–145 From Haydn's manuscripts in the Est. Coll. (now Budapest, Nat. Lib., Music Dept.) drawn by Dorrit Somfai-Révész. (Reduction 1 : 3.)

146 From the parts of *Giulio Sabino* by Sarti. Budapest, Nat. Lib., Music. Dept. OE-32.

147. Budapest, Nat. Lib., Dept. for Theatrical History A. M. 1186.

148–151 From the Est. Coll. (now Budapest, Nat. Lib., Music Dept.). Nos. 148 and 150 are inserted arias by Haydn (Hoboken XXIVb: 5, 18), No. 151 the adaptation of an aria by Haydn to *I due supposti conti* by Cimarosa (Bartha–Somfai, Katalog III: 19).

152 *Quando la rosa*, Hoboken XXIVb: 3. Budapest, Nat. Lib., Music Dept.

153 Title-page to *Clavier- und Singstücke verschiedener Art, componiert... von Johann Wilhelm Hässler. Erste Sammlung* [Pieces for Piano and Songs of Various Kinds, Composed... by Johann Wilhelm Haessler. First Collection]. Erfurt, 1782. From Haydn's Library, now Budapest, Nat. Lib., Musical Dept.

154 From the opera by Salieri *La scuola de' gelosi* (Bartha–Somfai, Katalog III: 5). Budapest, Nat. Lib. Music Dept.

155 See Iconogr. No. **2.** p. 213. Budapest, Nat. Mus. 'Many people are delighted...', CCLN p. 28. 'You once again make me your debtor...', CCLN p. 31.

156 Engraving by Johann Ernst Mansfeld. Vienna, ÖNB.

157–159 From the part for first violin of the Quartet Hoboken III: 37, 41, 38. Budapest, Nat. Lib., Music Dept.

160 Engraving after a painting by Josef Christ. Vienna, ÖNB.

161 Hummel Edition, 1782. Coll. of Anthony van Hoboken, Ascona. 'As a great patron...', CCLN pp. 33–34.—To the words *auf eine gantz neue besondere art* [in a new and special way] great importance has been attributed by musical literature in the investigation and analysis of the development of Haydn's style since Sandberger (*Zur Geschichte der Haydnischen Streichquartetts, Gesammelte Aufsätze* [To the History of Haydn's String Quartets, Coll. Treatises] München, 1921). However, it is not unlikely that the businesslike composer used this phrase in order to increase interest, all the more so as the same words are almost exactly repeated in another letter, in which he offers copies of the parts of the same quartet (to J. C. Lavater in Zurich, 3. 12. 1781).

162 Engraving by Philipp Morghen after Camillo Paderni. Vienna, ÖNB.

163 Engraving. Vienna, ÖNB.

164 Engraving by Johann Georg Ringlin after Salomon Kleiner. Coll. of H. C. Robbins Landon, Buggiano/Vienna.

165 See Iconogr. No. **4.** p. 213 (Photo: Vienna, ÖNB).

'Nobly born...', CCLN. p. 48.

166 Engraving by Riedel after Johann Adamek, 1815. Vienna, ÖNB.

167 Engraving by Vincent Alloja after Elisabeth Vigée-Lebrun. Salzburg, Mozarteum.

168 Engraving by Hieronymus Löschenkohl. Vienna, ÖNB.

169 Engraving by James Neagle after Lawrence. London, Mansell Collection.

'Once when Haydn...', Griesinger p. 20.

170 Engraving by Johann Georg Mansfeld after Leonard Posch, 1789. Salzburg, Mozarteum.

171 Detail from the oil painting *The Mozart Family* by Johann Nepomuk della Croce, Winter 1780/81. Salzburg, Mozarteum.

172 Detail from an engraving *c.* 1820. Vienna, Mus. d. Stadt.

'I tell you...', *Mozart, Briefe und Aufzeichnungen* [Mozart, Letters and Notes]. Complete edition, published by the International Mozarteum Foundation, Salzburg, collected and with commentary by Wilhelm A. Bauer and Otto Erich Deutsch, 4 Vols. Kassel etc., 1962/63 (Bärenreiter), Vol. III, p. 373.

173 Drawn and engraved by Karl Schütz, 1781. Budapest, Nat. Mus.

174 Vienna, Artaria & Co., 1785. Vienna, GdMF.

175 See Iconogr. No. **3**, p. 213.

176 Engraving by Ignaz Unterberger. Vienna, ÖNB.—N. B. Not to be identified with Franz Bernhard von Kees, who kept a catalogue of the Haydn symphonies (*cf.* Larsen 3HK).

177 Oil (Photo: Vienna, ÖNB.)

178 Budapest, Nat. Lib., Music Dept.

179 Engraving by Giovanni Vitalba. Salzburg, Mozarteum.

180 Hoboken X: 12, 3, 5, 1, 4, 2. Budapest, Nat. Lib., Music Dept.

181 Engraving. Vienna, ÖNB.

'I send you herewith...', CCLN p. 41.

182 Engraving by Jacob Adam after Anton Graff, Vienna, 1793. Vienna, ÖNB.

183 Budapest, Nat. Lib., Music Dept.

'His Majesty, King of Prussia...', CCLN p. 61.— N. B. In his letter, Friedrich Wilhelm II did not thank Haydn for the string quartets dedicated to him, but for the symphonies Hoboken I: 82–87.

184 Oil by Philipp Friedrich Hetsch, *c.* 1790. Fürstlich Oettingen-Wallerstein'sche Bibliothek und Kunstsammlung, [Prince Oettingen-Wallerstein's Library and Collection], Harburg.

185 Engraving by Edma Quenedey, Paris, Bibliothèque Nationale.

'...Since I am sure...', CCLN p. 99.

186 Madrid, Prado (Photo: Coll. of H. C. Robbins Landon, Buggiano/Vienna). According to the kind suggestion of Anthony van Hoboken, the music seen on the picture is perhaps a work by Michael Haydn, *Cupido Cunctator*. In the editor's view, it is more likely that the painter was inspired by the song entitled 'Cupido' by Joseph Haydn and published by Artaria in 1781, or else the well-known name of Haydn happened to be connected with a fictitious song-title.

187–188 From Haydn's library, now Budapest, Nat. Lib., Music Dept.

'Long in Madrid...', Part of Canto V. Contemporary English translation, published in London in 1807 by John Belfour, Esq.

'It was approximately fifteen years ago...', after the German orig. from the edition published by Breitkopf & Härtel, 1801.

189 Copy by Johann Schellinger for the concert-master 'Sig. Luigi' Tomasini, 1790. Budapest, Nat. Lib., Music Dept. Ms. Mus. OK–11.

190 See Iconogr. No. **6**, p. 213.

'You ask me...', CCLN p. 73.

191 Drawn and engraved by Karl Schütz, 1790. Budapest. Nat. Mus.

192 Vienna, ÖNB.

'Most respected...', CCLN pp. 85–86.

193 Drawn and engraved by Emil Hütter, Vienna, Mus. d. Stadt (Photo: Vienna, ÖNB).

'Nobly born...', CCLN pp. 96–97.

194 Oil (see also p. 34).

Eisenstadt, Haydn-Museum (Photo: Vouk, Vienna).

'Nobly born, most esteemed...', CCLN pp. 98–99.

195 Vienna, Stadtbibliothek.

196 Vienna, Kunsthistorisches Museum (on loan from GdMF, Vienna).

'...This Sonata...', '...It's only a pity...', CCLN, pp. 105, 106.

197 Engraving by J. C. Leopold and Friedrich Bernhard Werner. Coll. of Endre Csatkai, Sopron.

198 See Iconogr. No. **5**, p. 213.

'I was astonished...', CCLN pp. 100–102, 106.

199 From the Est. Arch., now Budapest, Nat. Lib., Dept. for Theatrical History.—N. B. It is worth noting that six Italian singers received a higher monthly salary than *Kapellmeister* Haydn.

200 Photo: Vienna, ÖNB.

201 Drawn and engraved by Johann Ziegler. Budapest. Nat. Mus.

'Salomon...', Griesinger, p. 22.

202 Engraving by Georg Sigismund Facius after Thomas Hardy. Vienna, Mus. d. Stadt.

203 Incomplete oil painting by Joseph Lange, 1782/83? Salzburg, Mozarteum.

'Prince Anton granted permission...', Dies pp. 119–120.

'Mozart said to Haydn, at a happy meal...', Griesinger pp. 22–23.

Page 110
204 By Johann Gottfried Haid. Vienna, ÖNB.
205 Engraved by Friedrich Lieder. Budapest. Nat. Mus.
'The discharged musicians...', Dies pp. 118–119.
'Shortly before his departure...', Griesinger p. 23.

Page 111
206 From the engraving *Die erfreuliche Zusammenkunft des Erzherzogs Karl mit dem Prinzen Anton von Sachsen zu Prag im Monat August 1800* [The happy meeting of Archduke Karl with Prince Anton of Saxony in Prague in August 1800]. Vienna, ÖNB.
207 Engraving by Egid Verhelst, 1799. Mannheim, Städtisches Schlossmuseum.

Page 112
208 Pen-and-ink drawing by Joseph Widnmann [*sic*], c. 1790. Fürstlich Oettingen-Wallerstein'sche Bibliothek und Kunstsammlung, Harburg.
209 Engraving. Vienna, ÖNB.
'In the capital...', Dies p. 121.

Page 113
210 Hand-coloured lithograph by William Daniell, 1805 (Photo: Coll. of H. C. Robbins Landon, Buggiano/Vienna).
'Most noble...', CCLN p. 113.

Page 114
211–212 Title-page and page 13. From Haydn's library, now Budapest, Nat. Lib., Music Dept. Ha. I. 15.

Page 115
213 Drawing (coloured in watercolour) by Thomas Hosmer Shepherd, 1831. London, British Museum (Photo: Coll. of H. C. Robbins Landon, Buggiano/Vienna).
'My arrival...', CCLN p. 112.

Page 116
214 See Iconogr. No. **7a**, p. 213 (Photo: Vienna, ÖNB).
215 London, British Museum.

Page 117
216 Engraving by J. Jagg (?) after E. Dayes, 1797. London, Mansell Collection.
217 Engraving. London, Mansell Collection.

Page 118
218 Engraving. London, Mansell Collection.
219 Painting by Thomas Lawrence. Windsor, Royal Collection (Photo: London, Mansell Collection).
'On 5th Nov...', CCLN pp. 251–253.

Page 119
220 Engraving. London, Mansell Collection.
221 Engraving by Leonard Heinrich Hessel, 1789. Vienna, ÖNB.
'I had to...', CCLN p. 274.

Page 120
222–223 Budapest, Nat. Lib., Music Dept.

Page 121
224 Engraving by William John Walker after John Dixon. London, British Museum.

Page 122
225 Engraving by Thomas Rowles and Robert Carver, publ. 1794. London, British Museum.
'8 days before Pentecost...', 'A gang of rowdy fellows...', CCLN, pp. 261 and 278.

Page 123
226 Engraving. London, British Museum.
227 Terracotta model by Louis-François Roubiliac.

(Müller-Blattau: *Georg Friedrich Händel. Der Wille zur Vollendung*. Mainz, 1959, Schott's Söhne.)
'Today, 4th June...', CCLN p. 262.

Page 124
228 See Iconogr. No. **8a**, p. 213 (Photo: Leipzig, Musikbibliothek der Stadt).
'I asked him...', Griesinger p. 33.

Page 125
229 See Iconogr. No. **8b**, p. 214 (Photo: R.B. Fleming and Co., London).
'When Haydn...', Dies p. 131.

Page 126
230 Drawing, 1800. London, Mansell Collection.
231 Budapest, Nat. Lib., Music Dept. Ms. Mus. I. 7.

Page 127
232–233 Two silhouettes by Hieronymus Löschenkohl. Vienna, ÖNB and Mus. d. Stadt, respectively.
234 Budapest, Nat. Lib., Music Dept. Ms. Mus. I. 18c.

Page 128
235 Engraving. London, British Museum (Photo: London, Mansell Collection).
236 Engraving after Joshua Reynolds. New York, Lennox Gallery (Photo: London, Mansell Collection).
237 Engraving by John Collyer after Philip Jean, 1794. London, British Museum.
'During his first eighteen months' stay...', Dies pp. 138–139.

Page 129
238 Published by John Bland, 1793. Vienna, ÖNB.
239 Painted and engraved by Thomas Hardy, Vienna, ÖNB.
240 Engraving by Johann Georg Mansfeld. Collection of Christa Landon, Vienna.
'Today, 14th January...', 'On 1st June...', CCLN pp. 255, 258–259.

Page 130
241 Engraving by James Godby after Friedrich Rehberg (1814). Vienna, ÖNB.
'On 15th June...', CCLN pp. 254–255.

Page 131
242 Engraving by H. S. Storer. London, British Museum.
'I passed through...', CCLN p. 272.

Page 132
243 Engraving by John Collyer after John Russell, 1792. London, British Museum.

Page 133
244 Engraving. London, Mansell Collection.
'I must take this opportunity...', CCLN pp. 123–124.

Page 134
245 See Iconogr. No. **9**, p. 214.

Page 135
246 Engraving by Biosse (Georges Louis Beausse) after Pierre-Narcis Guérin. Paris, Bibliothèque Nationale.
'...I never in my life wrote...', CCLN p. 128.
'...For some time I was...', CCLN p. 125.

Page 136
247 See Iconogr. No. **10a**, p. 214 (Photo: A. C. K. Ware Ltd., London).

Page 137
248 See Iconogr. No. **10b**, p. 214 (Photo: Vienna, ÖNB).

Page 138
249 Engraving. Budapest, Nat. Mus.
250 Oil. Est. Coll. (Photo: Coll. of H. C. Robbins Landon, Buggiano/Vienna).
'My dear Polzelli!...', CCLN p. 136.

345 See Iconogr. No. **24**, p. 217 (Coll. of Anthony van Hoboken, Ascona).

346 Picture engraved by Carl Heinrich Grünler after Bach. From Haydn's library, now Budapest, Nat. Lib., Music Dept.

347 Lithograph. London, British Museum.

348 From Haydn's library, now Budapest, Nat. Lib., Music Dept.

'Most esteemed Sir!...', CCLN p. 229.

349 Budapest, Nat. Lib., Music Dept. Ha. I. 2.

350 See Iconogr. No. **19**, p. 216 (Photo: Coll. of C.-G. Stellan-Mörner, Stockholm).

351 Oil by Hans Hansen, 1802. Coll. of the Silverstolpe family, Näs (Sweden).

352 Budapest, Nat. Lib., Music Dept.

353–354 By Karl Leberecht. After Haydn's death, it passed into the Est. Coll. (Photo: Robert Forstner, Eisenstadt).

355 Engraving by Ch. Meder after F. B. Kietz. Vienna, ÖNB.

'My dear Papa!...', CCLN p. 243.

356 Copy by Johann Elssler. From Haydn's library, now Budapest, Nat. Lib., Music Dept. Ha. I. 19.

357 Engraving by Sebastian Langer. Vienna, ÖNB.

358 Lithograph by Franz Eybl. Vienna, ÖNB.

359–361 Details. The ninth on the second page is the tenor Johann Haydn, Esterházy Archives, Eisenstadt (Photo: Coll. of H. C. Robbins Landon, Buggiano/Vienna).

362 Budapest, Nat. Lib., Dept. for Theatrical History.

363 See Iconogr. No. **26**, p. 217 (Photo: Robert Forstner, Eisenstadt).—N. B. The features on pictures Nos. 358 and 363 though not identical, are strikingly similar (Michael Haydn and—allegedly—Joseph Haydn) which suggests that pastel 363, of very doubtful authenticity, may have been a portrait of Michael Haydn.

364 Budapest, Nat. Lib., Music Dept., Ha. I. 8.

365 Vienna, GdMF.

366–368 Budapest, Nat. Lib., Music Dept. Ha. I. 5, 4, 6.

369 Budapest, Nat. Lib., Music Dept. Ha. I. 1.

370 Engraving by François Pigeot after Hippolyte Lecomte. Vienna, Mus. d. Stadt (Photo: Vienna, ÖNB).

371 Engraving, published by Weigl, Vienna. Vienna, ÖNB.—N. B. One copy of Cherubini's funeral music is in the Nat. Lib., Budapest, Music Dept. (formerly Est. Arch.).

372 From Haydn's library, now Budapest, Nat. Lib., Music Dept.

373 Engraving by Friedrich Fleischmann after F. H.

Müller (1822). Budapest, Nat. Mus.

'Dearest Hummel ...', CCLN p. 233.

'Most beloved Papa!...', CCLN p. 234.

374 1809. Est. Coll. (Photo: Vienna, Niederösterreichisches Landesmuseum).

375 Carpani holds his Haydn biography in his hand. Steel engraving. Vienna, ÖNB.

376 Lithograph after C. Rohrich, mid-19th century. Budapest, Nat. Mus.

377 Engraving by J. Dirnbacher after Lanzadelli, inscribed *Anton Polzelli / Zögling Jos. Haydn's und Fürstlich-Esterházyscher Musik-Director* [Pupil of Jos. Haydn and Prince Esterházy's Director of Music], with a handwritten note: *Aus Hochachtung, und Verehrung gewidmet—Pesth, 1878.—Emilie u. Antonia Polzelli.—Geschwister Polzelli, Enkelinen Haydn's.*—[Dedicated with esteem and respect—Pest, 1878.—Emilie and Antonia Polzelli.—Polzelli Sisters, Haydn's grand-daughters.] (Photo: Coll. of H. C. Robbins Landon, Buggiano/Vienna.)

'My dear Son!...', CCLN p. 244.

378 Drawn and engraved by Johann Ziegler. Budapest, Nat. Mus.

379 Vienna, Archiv der Stadt.

'In the name...', Vernon Gotwals: 'Joseph Haydn's Last Will and Testament.' *Musical Quarterly* XLVII (1961), pp. 331–353.

380 Formerly in the Esterházy Archives, destroyed during the war (Photo: Larsen 3HK).

381 See Iconogr. No. **20**, p. 216. Vienna, Est. Arch. (Photo: Collection of Johann Harich, Eisenstadt).

382 See Iconogr. No. **21**, p. 216 (Photo: Budapest, Nat. Mus.).

383 Drawn and engraved by Karl Schütz, 1790. Budapest, Nat. Mus.

384 See Iconogr. No. **22**, p. 216 (Photo: Vienna, ÖNB).

385 Oil. Est. Coll. (Photo: Coll. of H. C. Robbins Landon, Buggiano/Vienna).

386 *Cf.* picture 384.

387 Engraving by François Aubertin after Alexandre Delaborde. Vienna, ÖNB.

388 Engraving by F. Lorzing after Ferdinand Jagemann (1812). Vienna, Mus. d. Stadt.

389 Engraving by Benedikt Piringer after Johann Nepomuk Stöckle. Vienna, ÖNB.

390 Drawing. Burgenländisches Landesmuseum (Haydn-Haus, Eisenstadt). (Photo: Coll. of H. C. Robbins Landon, Buggiano/Vienna.)

391 Vienna, Archiv der Stadt.

392 Vienna, GdMF.

393 See Iconogr. No. **23**, p. 217 (Photo: Vienna, ÖNB).

394 From the Est. Arch., now Budapest, Nat. Lib., Music Dept., Ha. I. 9.

# INDEX

## (A) LIST OF WORKS BY HAYDN MENTIONED
### (ACCORDING TO HOBOKEN-NUMBERS)

The Index includes all references to titles of works, names, places and technical terms, except the literature (title, publisher, place of publishing) quoted in the Commentaries.

The numbers in angle brackets ⟨ ⟩ refer to the numbering of the picture section (pages 1–208) and at the same time indicate that the object or person is not only mentioned but there is a picture as well.

The list of works by Haydn that have been mentioned are put into sequence according to the numbers used in the thematic index by Dr. H. C. Anthony van Hoboken *(Joseph Haydn, Thematisch-bibliographisches Werkverzeichnis)* Volume I *(Instrumentalwerke)* Mainz, 1957. The numbers of Volume II *(Vokalwerke)* not yet published when this book was in preparation, have been kindly supplied by Dr. van Hoboken.

## (B) GENERAL INDEX (PERSONS, PLACES, THINGS)